Spanish
Grammar Buster

Tony Buzan and
Carmen García del Río

First published 2010
by Collins an imprint of

HarperCollins Publishers
77-85 Fulham Palace Road
London
W6 8JB

www.collinslanguage.com

10 9 8 7 6 5 4 3 2 1 0

© HarperCollins Publishers 2010

ISBN 978-0-00-730305-2

A catalogue record for this book is available
from the British Library

Edited by Huw Jones
Design by Q2AMedia & Anthony Smith

Typeset by Davidson Publishing Solutions, Glasgow

Printed in India by Gopsons Papers Ltd

Contents

How to use this book

Contents

How to use this book

You may know your vocabulary off by heart, but vocabulary without grammar is just about as useful as a car without wheels or a bird without wings! Learn how to really kick your Spanish into action with the **Spanish Grammar Buster**.

Set out in an easy-to-follow format, we've divided the book into 20 colourful units, each clearly explaining a separate grammar point. As we don't use any confusing or complicated jargon, you'll soon find that learning these basic principles is simple and will not only dramatically improve your written and spoken Spanish but will increase your confidence when approaching grammar in the future. Crosswords, word searches, anagrams and Mind Maps make learning grammar fun while Tony Buzan's tried and tested memory techniques will mean you'll always remember what you've learnt. If you don't believe us, then all you have to do is try out our mental gymnastics exercises to put your new found skills to the test – you'll be surprised by just how fast you progress! Any unfamiliar terms will be explained in the glossary (if you see a G after a word, it is referring you to the glossary for further information) and a handy pocket-sized verb wheel means you'll be grammar-perfect at home and away. The answers are all at the back of the book for easy reference.

How it works

We've based this book on the principles of ASSOCIATION, IMAGINATION and MIND-MAPPING. We use this method because *we remember best when we associate what we learn with something we already know*.

Mind Maps®

Mind Maps are one of the best thinking tools available. Some Mind Maps are already drawn for you to help you visualise and retain new information but the best Mind Maps are those you make yourself. Feel free to add new branches to the Mind Maps in the book as you increase your vocabulary, or make a new Mind Map with words important to you.

To make a Mind Map® follow these simple steps:

Step one: Take a blank piece of paper and some coloured pens. Turn the page to landscape format, to make a wide rectangle. In the middle, draw an image of what your Mind Map is about: for example, if it is about food, draw something delicious.

Step two: Next draw branches coming out in all directions from your central image, one for each main group of words.

Step three: Connect second-level branches to the first, and third-level branches to those. Make your branches curves rather than straight lines and use colours and images throughout.

Go to **www.collinslanguage.com/revolution** to find out more about Mind Mapping.

Repeat and Succeed!

Learning a foreign language means first understanding, then learning and finally remembering. Revision is therefore essential.

The specific formula for fixing information in your long-term memory is:
- **1st repetition** – an hour or so after first learning it
- **2nd repetition** – a day later
- **3rd repetition** – a week later
- **4th repetition** – a month later
- **5th repetition** – six months later

Rest and Learn Best

You will find it easier to retain information if you *take regular breaks between study periods*. During breaks your brain will naturally and spontaneously integrate what it has learnt.

Your brain finds it easier to remember more from the start and end of study periods than from the middle. Regular breaks cut the amount of time in the middle of study sessions.

You are now ready to get to grips with grammar!

We hope you have fun!

How to name people, animals and things

In this unit you'll find out that Spanish nouns have a gender.

Nouns have gender

Naming words for people, animals, objects and ideas are called **nouns** (G). Nouns are either **feminine** (G – see Gender) or **masculine** (G – see Gender) in Spanish. You'll find the **gender** (G) given in the dictionary, but below there are some clues to help you work out the gender of Spanish nouns for yourself. There is some logic to it – at least for people and animals!

People and animals

The gender of most nouns referring to people and animals coincides with their biological gender. So most nouns referring to male human beings and male animals are masculine and most nouns referring to female human beings and female animals are feminine.

Masculine		**Feminine**	
hombre	man	mujer	woman
abuel**o**	grandfather	abuel**a**	grandmother
caballo	stallion	yegua	mare
per**ro**	(male) dog	per**ra**	(female) dog, bitch

People
Some 'people' words have only one gender, no matter whether you are talking about a man or a woman:

Always masculine		**Always feminine**	
bebé	baby boy or baby girl	**persona**	male or female person
personaje	character (in a book/film)	**víctima**	victim
genio	genius	**estrella**	TV/film star

Animals

Some words for animals don't change according to the sex of the animal.
There's no pattern to these: you just have to learn the Spanish word with its gender,
which is always the same.

Always masculine

cocodrilo crocodile
chimpancé chimpanzee

These are always masculine – even if you
are talking about a female crocodile,
or chimpanzee.

If you want to refer to the sex of an
animal, you have to add the nouns
macho (male) or **hembra** (female)
to the name of the animal:
ballena macho
ballena hembra

Always feminine

tortuga tortoise
girafa giraffe
ballena whale

These are always feminine – even if
you are talking about a male tortoise,
giraffe or whale.

To remember that these words are
feminine, picture a tortoise wearing a
flowery hat, a giraffe with a flower
behind its ear – or a whale wearing
a tutu!

Summary:

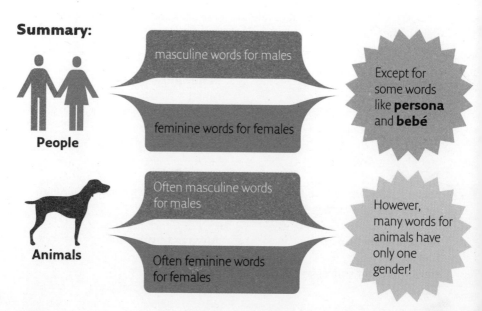

People — masculine words for males / feminine words for females — Except for some words like **persona** and **bebé**

Animals — Often masculine words for males / Often feminine words for females — However, many words for animals have only one gender!

How to turn a masculine word into a feminine one and vice versa

Sometimes the masculine and the feminine nouns are very different, like **hombre** and **mujer**, **caballo** and **yegua**. However, in other instances you can turn the masculine word you find in the dictionary into a feminine one by changing the ending. The main patterns are:

Masculine nouns	Feminine form	
For most nouns ending in −o	Replace the −o with an −a	abuelo (grandfather), abuela (grandmother), gato (male cat), gata (female cat). Some words are invariable: piloto (pilot/racing driver), modelo (model)
Nouns ending in −or	Add an −a to the masculine form	profesor (male teacher), profesora (female teacher)
Nouns ending in −ón, −ín, −és	Change to −ona, −ina, −esa respectively	campeón (male champion), campeona (female champion), bailarín (male dancer), bailarina (female dancer)
Nouns ending in −e or a **consonant** other than those already mentioned	Many of them remain the same	adolescente (adolescent), cantante (singer), joven (youth), líder (leader). Some exceptions are: jefe/jefa (boss), dependiente/dependienta (shop assistant), pariente/parienta (relative)
Nouns ending in −a	Remain the same	artista (artist), dentista (dentist), astronauta (astronaut), atleta (athlete)

Mental gymnastics 1

Match the masculine noun with its feminine equivalent.

padre   yerno   marido   gallo   toro   macho   rey

hembra   vaca   nuera   reina   madre   mujer   gallina

Mental gymnastics 2

Write the feminine form of the following nouns.

1 tío _tía_
2 tenista _tenista_
3 león _leona_
4 panda _panda_

5 intérprete _intérprete_
6 amigo _amiga_
7 estudiante _estudiante_
8 perro _perra_

Things

Objects that you can see and touch such as 'table' or 'house' – even abstract things like 'beauty', 'history' or 'decision' – all have a gender in Spanish. The gender of these nouns has nothing to do with their being male or female. Remember, all nouns in Spanish are either masculine or feminine.

Dictionaries indicate the genders of nouns. There are also some rules to help you work out the gender. In general, most nouns ending in **-o** are masculine: **libro** (book) and most nouns ending in **-a** are feminine: **falda** (skirt). However, there are some exceptions to this rule, the most important ones being:

Masculine nouns ending in -a: **día** (day), **clima** (climate), **idioma** (language), **mapa** (map), **planeta** (planet), **problema** (problem), **programa** (programme).

Feminine nouns ending in -o: **mano** (hand), **foto** – short for **fotografía** (photograph), **moto** – short for **motocicleta** (motorcycle).

Many nouns do not end in either **-o** or **-a**. The following rules can help you to decide the gender of a noun.

Nouns that are usually feminine

Nouns ending in **-dad**, **-tad** and **-ud** — **ciudad** (city), **libertad** (liberty/freedom), **salud** (health)

Nouns ending in **-ión** — **acción** (action), **estación** (station), **pasión** (passion)
Two exceptions: **avión** (aeroplane) and **camión** (lorry)

| Names of letters are feminine | **la a**, **la be**, **la ce**, **la de** (a, b, c, d) |

Nouns that are usually masculine

Nouns ending in **-ón**	**jamón** (ham), **melón** (melon)
Nouns ending in **-or**	**amor** (love), **motor** (motor)
Nouns ending in **-aje**	**garaje** (garage), **paisaje** (landscape)
Nouns ending in a stressed vowel	**sofá** (sofa), **plató** (cinema set)
Names of the days	**el lunes** (Monday), **el martes** (Tuesday), **el miércoles** (Wednesday)
Names of languages	**el español** (Spanish), **el inglés** (English)
Names of rivers, seas and oceans	**el Támesis** (the Thames), **el Mediterráneo**, **el Atlántico**
Names of colours	**el rojo** (red), **el azul** (blue)

The gender of nouns ending in **-e** or those that do not follow any of the above patterns is not so easy to predict, so when you're learning new vocabulary learn the gender of nouns at the same time: **coche** (car) is masculine but **noche** (night) is feminine; **hotel** (hotel) is masculine but **nariz** (nose) is feminine.

Tony's Tip

Masculine or feminine?

An easy, fun way to remember whether a Spanish word is masculine or feminine is to pick a super-masculine figure and associate him with every masculine word. Do the same with the feminine words and a super-feminine figure.

Suppose you've chosen El Zorro as your masculine figure and a female flamenco dancer, called Lola as the feminine one.

For **hotel**, imagine El Zorro riding his horse into the lobby of a luxury hotel and picking up the room key with his sword.
For **estación**, picture Lola dancing the flamenco as your train pulls in.

Mental gymnastics 3

Here is a list of Spanish words, which are very similar to English. Try to guess their gender with the help of the explanations on the previous page. Write **m** or **f** after each word.

1	excursión	...f.....	10	clima	...M...
2	problema	...M....	11	región	...M...
3	terraza	...f.....	12	garaje	..m....
4	universidad	...f.....	13	cultura	...f....
5	limón	..M....	14	profesora	....f....
6	doctor	...m....	15	sardina	...f....
7	cine	..M....	16	biquini	...f.....
8	altitud	...f.....	17	inglés	..m....
9	Pacífico	..m.....	18	diversidad	...f......

Mental gymnastics 4

Sort the following nouns into masculine (m) and feminine (f) groups.

**gato · mujer · mano · arroz · mesa · libro · avión · martes
amarillo · niña · cantante · cocina · moto · día · hermana
problema · noche · marido**

masculine (m)	feminine (f)
gat	mujer
	Mano

How to make nouns plural

As with gender, there are certain rules that will help you make the plural form of Spanish nouns. The table below summarises these rules.

Formation of the plural

Singular nouns ending in a vowel (**a, e, i, o, u, á, é, ó**)	Add **-s**	cama cama**s** hombre hombre**s** sofá sofá**s**
Singular nouns ending in a consonant, or **-í** or **-ú**	Add **-es**	profesor profesor**es** iraní (Iranian) iraní**es** exceptions: champú (shampoo) champú**s**, menú (menu) menú**s**
Nouns ending in a **-z** in the singular	Change the **-z** to **-c** in the plural	luz (light) lu**ces** (lights)
Nouns which have an accent in the last syllable	Lose the accent in the plural	inglés ingle**ses** región regi**ones**
Nouns ending in an unstressed vowel plus **-s**	No change	lunes (Monday/Mondays)

Masculine plural
The masculine plural denotes either a group of males, or a mixture of males and females:

niños   =   a group of boys/a group of boys and girls

hermanos   =   brothers/brothers and sisters

estudiantes   =   a group of male students/a group of male and female students

padres   =   fathers/parents

Mental gymnastics 5

Guess the plural form of the following words. Take care with the accents!

**limón · café · hindú · mesa · mujer · paz · familia · hotel · taxi
ballena · autobús · miércoles**

-s	-es		no change
....	....	....	....
....	....	....	....
....	....	....	....

Mental gymnastics 6

Translate the following words into Spanish. Use a dictionary if you're not sure of a particular word.

1   grandparents   ....
2   male and female cousins ....
3   sons and daughters   ....
4   uncle(s) and aunt(s)   ....

Special cases

- **nouns** for things you cannot count such as **pan** (bread), **agua** (water),
  vino (wine), **azúcar** (sugar) are used in the **singular** to talk about things in
  general or an unspecified amount. When the **plural** is used it refers to different
  types or various units of the same thing:

singular: ¿Bebes vino en las comidas?
             Do you drink wine with your meals? (wine, a type of drink)
plural: Tengo vinos de gran calidad.
             I have wines of great quality (different types of wine).
             Tomo dos vinos al día.
             I drink two glasses of wine per day (several glasses of wine).

- Some nouns in the **singular** refer to groups with various members:
  familia (family), **gente** (people), **público** (public), **ropa** (clothes), **policía** (police). These nouns are often or always treated as plural in English:
  la familia es ... the family are ...
  la gente es ... people are ...
  el público tiene ... the public have ...

- Other nouns are normally used in the plural:
  gafas (de sol) ((sun)glasses), **prismáticos** (binoculars), **tijeras** (scissors), **zapatos** (shoes).

Mental gymnastics 7

Sort the following nouns into singular, plural, and singular nouns referring to groups.

persona · tijeras · abuelos · ropa · perro · zapatos · sal · familia
sábado · menús · hijo · gente · gafas · canguro

singular	plural	singular nouns referring to groups
....	....	....
....	....	....
....	....	....
....	....	
....	....	
....		

How to say
the, *a* and *some*

2

How to say 'the'

In Spanish there are four words for 'the'. The words for 'the' in the **singular** (G – see
Number) are **el** (masculine) and **la** (feminine).

- **el** is used before a masculine and singular noun and **la** is used before a feminine
  singular noun.
- Use **el** or **la** when referring to something specific.

el niño the boy	**la** niña the girl
el estudiante the male student	**la** estudiante the female student
el león lion	**la** leona lioness

masculine
singular 'the'
el

feminine
singular 'the'
la

Some points to remember
- Many nouns ending in **-e** or a **consonant** have the same form for males and
  females; to differentiate the gender use **el** for males and **la** for females before the
  noun:

el estudiante (the male student)	**la** estudiante (the female student)
el joven (the male youth)	**la** joven (the female youth)

- Before feminine singular nouns starting with stressed **a** or **ha** the form **el** is used:
  el agua (the water)   **el** águila (the eagle)   **el** hacha (the axe)

- The prepositions **a** and **de**, when followed by **el** become a single word:
  a + el = al   de + el = del

Mental gymnastics 1

Write **el** or **la** before each of the following nouns. Some have been done for you.

1	..... ordenador	7	..... mermelada	13	..... pantalón
2	..... artículo	8	..... persona	14	..... camión
3	..... agua	9	..... hombre	15	..,.. bebé
4	**el** profesor	10	..... chocolate	16	..... paella
5	**la** tortuga	11	..... hija		
6	..... cerveza	12	..... Himalaya		

When you learn a new noun, always learn it with the word for 'the' that goes with it (**el** or **la**), as this will help you to remember the gender of the noun.

How to say 'a'

The Spanish words for 'a' are: **un** (masculine) and **una** (feminine).

- **un** is used before a masculine singular noun and **una** is used before a feminine singular noun.
- Use **un** or **una** when referring to something unspecific.

masculine 'a'
un

feminine 'a'
una

Some points to remember

- many nouns ending in **-e** or a **consonant** have the same form for males and females; to differentiate the gender use **un** for males and **una** for females before the noun:

un estudiante (a male student)   **una** estudiante (a female student)
un joven (a male youth)   **una** joven (a female youth)

- before feminine singular nouns starting with stressed **a** or **ha** the form **un** is used:

un agua (a water)
un águila (an eagle)
un hacha (an axe)

Mental gymnastics 2

Solve the anagrams to find some of the nouns from Unit 1 preceded by **un** or **una**.

1	NAU MEUJR		4	NU BPOLRAME	
2	NU LOLACBA		5	NUA NOAM	
3	NUA GAMIA		6	NU CEHCO	

Mental gymnastics 3

Fill in the missing letters to find some more nouns from Unit 1 preceded by **el**, **la**, **un** or **una**.

1	.....l h.....mb.....		4	l..... p..... .....so....., ...	
2	.....n..... l..... .....n.....		5	.....l a..... .....a	
3	e..... r..... ....n		6	.....n..... u.....i..... .....r..... .....d.....d	

How to say the plural 'the'

The Spanish words for the **plural** (**G** – see Number) 'the' are **los** (masculine plural) and **las** (feminine plural).

- **los** is used before a masculine plural noun and **las** is used before a feminine plural noun.
- Use **los** or **las** when referring to something specific.
  los niños the boys   **las niñas** the girls
  los leones the lions   **las leonas** the lionesses

masculine plural
'the' **los**

feminine plural
'the' **las**

Some points to remember

- many nouns ending in **-e** or a **consonant** have the same form for males and females; to differentiate the gender use **los** for males and **las** for females before the noun:
  los estudiantes (the male students)   **las** estudiantes (the female students)
  los jóvenes (the male youths)   **las** jóvenes (the female youths)

- before feminine plural nouns starting with stressed **a** or **ha** the form **las** is used:
  las aguas (the waters)
  las águilas (the eagles)
  las hachas (the axes)

Mental gymnastics 4

Write the name of the item illustrated. Include **el**, **la**, **los**, **las** as appropriate.

1

2

3

4

5

6

1	....	4	....
2	....	5	....
3	....	6	....

Mental gymnastics 5

Write these nouns in plural form, including **los** and **las** as appropriate. Take care with the accents!

1	noche	....	5	melón	....
2	jueves	....	6	foto	....
3	problema	....	7	avión	....
4	persona	....			

How to say 'some' or 'any'

The Spanish words for 'some' are: **unos** (masculine) and **unas** (feminine).

- **unos** is used before a masculine plural noun and **unas** is used before a feminine plural noun.
- use **unos** or **unas** when referring to something unspecific.

masculine
'some' or 'any'

unos

feminine
'some' or 'any'

unas

Some points to remember

- many nouns ending in **-e** or a **consonant** have the same form for males and females; to differentiate the gender use **unos** for males and **unas** for females before the noun:

unos estudiantes	**unas** estudiantes
(some male students)	(some female students)
unos jóvenes	**unas** jóvenes
(some male youths)	(some female youths)

- before feminine plural nouns starting with stressed **a** or **ha** the form **unas** is used:
  unas aguas (some waters)
  unas águilas (some eagles)
  unas hachas (some axes)

Mental gymnastics 6

Write these nouns in plural form, including **unos** and **unas** as
appropriate:

1	persona	5	día	....
2	camión	6	vaca	....
3	águila	7	moto	....
4	hotel			

Mental gymnastics 7

Fill in the missing letters to find some more words from Unit 1 preceded
by **un**, **una**, **unos** or **unas**.

1	.....n g.....t.....	4	u..... ..... h..... .....a
2	.....n..... a..... ig.....	5	u..... .....s s..... .....á.....
3	.....n.....s p.....r..... .....s	6	.....no..... e..... .....u.....ia.....t.....s

How to describe someone or something 3

In this unit, you'll learn how to talk about the appearance, colour, characteristics, character or nationality of people and objects.

Adjectives: describing words

Adjectives (G) are words that describe **nouns** (G). When we talk about the appearance or the characteristics of someone or something we use words such as **alto** (tall), **grande** (big), **redondo** (round) or **simpático** (nice). So when we say **Juan es simpático** (Juan is nice) or **la mesa es redonda** (the table is round), the words **simpático** and **redonda** give us more information about Juan and the table.

Spanish adjectives agree in gender and in number with the nouns they describe. They become masculine or feminine and singular or plural to match the people or the things that they describe:

un hombre alt**o**
unos hombres alto**s**

una mujer alt**a**
unas mujeres alta**s**

When a masculine noun and a feminine noun share the same adjective, the adjective takes the masculine plural form:

un hombre y una mujer altos

Formation of the feminine

Masculine adjectives ending in	Feminine form	Masculine	Feminine
-o	Replace the -o with an -a	alto simpático redondo	alta (tall) simpática (nice) redonda (round)
vowels other than -o (a, e, i, u)	Remains the same	grande egoísta	grande (big) egoísta (selfish)
consonant	Remains the same	joven fácil	joven (young) fácil (easy)
-ón, -ín, -án, -or	Replace with -ona, -ina, -ana and -ora	dormilón parlanchín holgazán trabajador	dormilona (sleepyhead) parlanchina (talkative) holgazana (lazy) trabajadora (hard-working)

Mental gymnastics 1

Write the feminine version of the following phrases. Take care with the accents!

Example: **un hombre alto**   **una mujer alta**

1	un gato bonito	....
2	un niño dormilón	....
3	un atleta joven	....
4	un marido inteligente	....
5	un estudiante hablador	....

Mental gymnastics 2

Write the feminine version of the following adjectives.

1	nervioso	....	6	difícil	....
2	impaciente	....	7	optimista	....
3	pesimista	....	8	atractivo	....
4	alegre	....	9	importante	....
5	trabajador	....	10	feliz	....

Formation of the plural

masculine and feminine forms ending in vowel add **-s**

alto alto**s**
redonda redonda**s**
grande grande**s**

Plural of describing words

masculine and feminine forms ending in consonant add **-es**

fácil fácil**es**

(adjectives ending in -**z** in the singular change the -**z** to -**c** in the plural)

feli**z** feli**ces**

Mental gymnastics 3

Write the plural form of the following adjectives.

1	tranquilo	....	5	holgazán	....
2	delgada	....	6	fuerte	....
3	organizada	....	7	capaz	....
4	gordo	....	8	intelectual	....

Mental gymnastics 4

How would you say these phrases in Spanish?

1   an interesting city   ....
2   a round suitcase   ....
3   a grey mouse   ....
4   a tall man   ....
5   a big baby   ....
6   a pretty actress   ....

Nationality words

Words like **español** (Spanish) and **británico** (British) are used to describe the
nationality of someone or something. As with any other Spanish adjectives,
Spanish words for nationality agree in gender and in number with the nouns they
describe. They become **masculine**, **feminine**, **singular** or **plural** like the
people, or the things they are describing:

un hombre inglés   **una** mujer inglesa
unos hombres ingleses   **unas** mujeres inglesas

As we saw before, when a masculine noun and a feminine noun share the same
adjective, the adjective takes the masculine plural form:

un hombre y una mujer ingleses

Formation of the feminine

Masculine adjectives ending in	Feminine form	Masculine	Feminine
-o	Replace the -o with an -a	colombiano australiano	colombiana australiana

consonant	Add –**a**. If there is an accent on the final vowel, remove it.	español inglés neozelandés	español**a** ingles**a** neozeland**esa**
–**e**, –**a**, –**í** or –**ú**	Remains the same	canadiense estadounidense belga iraquí hindú	canadiense estadounidense belga iraquí hindú

Formation of the plural

Masculine and feminine adjectives ending in the singular in	Plural form	Singular	Plural
–**o**, –**e** or –**a**	Add –**s**.	colombiano canadiense estadounidense belga	colombiano**s** canadiense**s** estadounidense**s** belga**s**
consonant	Add –**es**. If there is an accent on the final vowel, remove it.	español inglés	español**es** ingl**eses**
–**í** or –**ú**	Add –**es**.	iraquí hindú	iraquí**es** hindú**es**

Mental gymnastics 5

Say whether the following nationalities refer to a man, a woman, or either.

1 japonés ....
2 española ....
3 belgas ....
4 china ....

5 iraníes ....
6 canadiense ....
7 alemanes ....
8 estadounidense ....

Mind Map it!

Complete the following Mind Map to remember what you have learned in Unit 3.

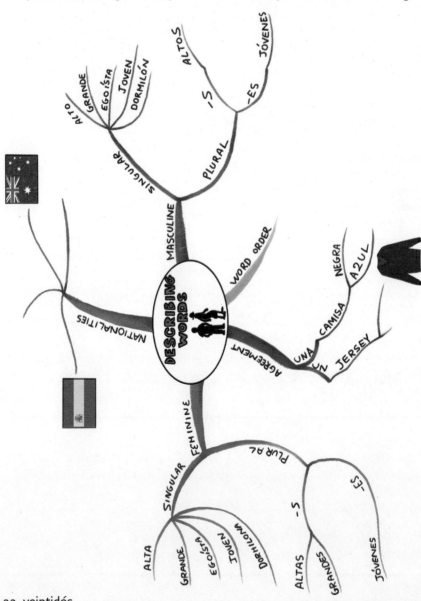

How to say *my, your, his, her, its, our* and *their* 4

In this unit, you will learn about one type of **possessive adjectives** (G).

Possessive adjectives

Possessive adjectives are words such as 'my', 'your', 'his' or 'her' which are used before a noun (G) to show that one person, animal, object or idea belongs to another.

In Spanish these words agree with their noun, i.e. they agree with what is possessed, not with the possessor.

For example, **su amigo** can mean 'his (male) friend' or 'her (male) friend' – the context makes it clear whether the speaker means 'his' or 'her'. Similarly, **su amiga** can either mean 'his' (female) friend or 'her' (female) friend'. In both instances, the possessive adjective is determined by 'friend' rather than whether the person to whom the friendship belongs is a man or woman.

my, your (singular), his, her, its and their

The Spanish forms equivalent to 'my', 'your' (singular), 'his', 'her', 'its' and 'their' agree with what is possessed in number only as the masculine and feminine forms are the same:

My son = **mi hijo**
(**hijo** is singular, so **mi** is singular too)
My sons = **mis hijos**
(**hijos** is plural, so **mis** is plural too)

My daughter = **mi hija**
(**hija** is singular, so **mi** is singular too)
My daughters = **mis hijas**
(**hijas** is plural, so **mis** is plural too)

our and your (plural, informal)

The forms for 'our' and 'your' (plural, informal) agree with what is possessed in number and **gender** (G) as they have different forms for the singular and the plural as well as for the masculine and the feminine.

Our son = **nuestro hijo**
(**hijo** is singular and masculine, so **nuestro** is singular and masculine too)
Our daughter = **nuestra hija**
(**hija** is singular and feminine, so **nuestra** is singular and feminine too)

Our sons = **nuestros hijos**
(**hijos** is plural and masculine, so **nuestros** is plural and masculine too)
Our daughters = **nuestras hijas**
(**hijas** is plural and feminine, so **nuestras** is plural and feminine too)

When you refer to a mix of male(s) and female(s) choose the plural of the masculine form:

Our uncle(s) and aunt(s) = **nuestros tíos**

| | singular | | plural | |
	masculine	**feminine**	**masculine**	**feminine**
my	**mi** hijo	**mi** hija	**mis** hijos	**mis** hijas
your (*sing. informal*)	**tu** hermano	**tu** hermana	**tus** hermanos	**tus** hermanas
your (*sing. formal*), his, her, its	**su** padre	**su** madre	**sus** padres	**sus** madres
our	**nuestro** sobrino	**nuestra** sobrina	**nuestros** sobrinos	**nuestras** sobrinas
your (*plural, informal*)	**vuestro** tío	**vuestra** tía	**vuestros** tíos	**vuestras** tías
your (*plural, formal*), their	**su** marido	**su** mujer	**sus** maridos	**sus** mujeres

The word for the formal form of 'your' is the same as the one for 'his', 'her', 'its' and 'their'.

There's no distinction between 'your' (formal & singular), 'his', 'her', 'its', 'your' (formal & plural) and 'their'. As you can see, the forms **su** and **sus** have several possible meanings, but normally in speech there is no ambiguity. However, if the meaning is unclear from the context, Spanish will use **de él**, **de ella**, **de usted**,

de ellos, **de ellas** or **de ustedes** (or **de** + name/thing) to avoid any confusion:

su padre	your (formal)/his/her/their father
el padre de él	his father
sus tías	your (formal)/his/her/their) aunts
la tía de ella	her aunt
su motor	its engine
el motor del coche	the car's engine

Expressing ownership or relationships

Spanish has no equivalent to the English **'s** to express ownership or relationships. Instead **de** (of) is used:

La amiga de Lola	Lola's friend (literally 'the friend of Lola')
el piso de Juan	Juan's flat

Mental gymnastics 1

Solve the anagrams to find some words to do with clothing preceded by possessive adjectives.

1 svotuesr zsopata ....
2 im laaóntnp ....
3 us aaldf ....
4 ut laceítnc ....
5 unsetar bausl ....
6 ssu btaos ....

Mental gymnastics 2

Match the Spanish and English equivalents. You can check in the previous units whether the words are masculine or feminine.

1	mi amigo	a	my children
2	su mesa	b	their motorbikes
3	tu coche	c	our sisters
4	nuestro problema	d	your car
5	mis hijos	e	your flat
6	sus motos	f	my friend
7	nuestras hermanas	g	her table
8	vuestro piso	h	our problem

Mental gymnastics 3

Write phrases using **de usted**, **de él**, **de ella**, **de ustedes**, **de ellos**, **de ellas**. Example: **your house → la casa de usted**

1   his photos   ....
2   your (formal, singular) keys   ....
3   her shoes   ....
4   their (Juan and María's) children   ....
5   their (Carmen and Elena's) husbands   ....

Mental gymnastics 4

Write the Spanish equivalent of the following phrases.

1   Claudia's email   ....
2   Pablo's bicycle   ....
3   my sister's husband   ....
4   your (informal, singular) parents' flats   ....
5   Elena's friends   ....

Mental gymnastics 5

Rewrite the following phrases using the example as a model.

Example: **mi sobrina y mi sobrino → mis sobrinos**

1   mi amiga y tu amiga   ....
2   su hermano y su hermana   ....
3   tu coche y mi coche   ....
4   mi hijo y mi hija   ....
5   tu moto y su moto   ....
6   su padre y su madre   ....
7   tu tío y tu tía   ....
8   mi moto y tu moto   ....

Mental gymnastics 6

Write the following phrases in Spanish.

1   our friends   ....
2   his mother   ....
3   your (formal, plural) son   ....
4   their house   ....
5   her niece and nephew   ....
6   your (informal, singular) parents   ....
7   our (female) cats   ....
8   my hands   ....
9   your (informal, plural) cars   ....
10   our baby   ....
11   your (informal, singular) book   ....
12   my (male) teacher   ....

How to say *mine, yours, his, hers, ours* and *theirs*

5

In this unit, you'll learn how to say 'mine', 'yours', 'his', 'hers', 'ours' and 'theirs'.

It's mine!

In Unit 4, you learnt how to say that something belongs to somebody using **possessive adjectives** (G), e.g. **mi(s)**, **tu(s)**, **su(s)**:

my car **mi coche**   my cars **mis coches**
your house **tu casa**   your houses **tus casas**

If you don't want to repeat the name of the possessed thing, you can just say 'mine', 'yours', 'his', 'hers' and so on. These words are called **possessive pronouns** (G).

In Spanish, these words have to agree in gender and number with the possessed thing, not with the person who possesses it.

So **mi coche** (my car) is replaced by **el mío** (mine) because **el coche** is masculine and singular. But **mi casa** (my house) is replaced by **la mía** (mine) because **la casa** is feminine and singular.

my car **mi coche → el mío**   my cars **mis coches → los míos**
my house **mi casa → la mía**   my houses **mis casas → las mías**

Let's look at this more closely:

mine, yours, his, her, our, yours, theirs
On the following pages you'll find the options for saying that something belongs to somebody. Just choose according to the gender and number of the possessed thing that you are talking about.

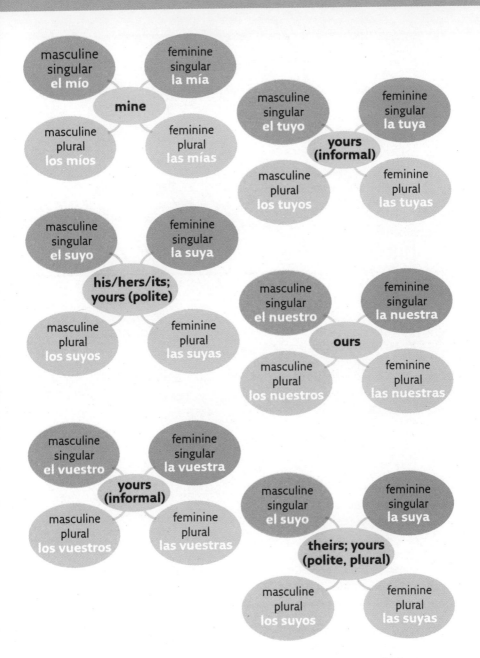

Mental gymnastics 1

Match each phrase in the left-hand column with the possessive pronouns in the right-hand column.

1	mis cosas	a	la tuya
2	su trabajo	b	el nuestro
3	tu jefa	c	las mías
4	vuestros ordenadores	d	el suyo
5	tus profesores	e	el mío
6	nuestro libro	f	los tuyos
7	sus tías	g	los vuestros
8	mi teléfono	h	las suyas

Mental gymnastics 2

Write the correct form of 'mine', 'yours', 'his/hers', 'ours' and 'theirs'.
Example: **su mano** – theirs → **la suya**

Remember! In Spanish 'mine', 'yours', 'his/hers', 'ours' and 'theirs' have to agree in gender and number with the possessed thing, not with the person who possesses it.

1	su maleta – hers	....
2	sus pasaportes – theirs	....
3	nuestros hijos – ours	....
4	mis padres – mine	....
5	tu hija – yours	....
6	su piso – yours (polite, singular)	....
7	sus llaves – his	....
8	nuestra habitación – ours	....
9	vuestros amigos – yours	....
10	sus problemas – yours (polite, plural)	....

Mental gymnastics 3

Fill in the missing letters to find some of the equivalents of 'mine', 'yours', 'his/hers', 'ours' and 'theirs'.

1 l..... m..... .....
2 .....l v..... ....tr.....
3 l..... s.....y.....

4 l.....s t..... .....as
5 ..... l s..... ....
6 l.....s n..... ....t .....o.....

Crystal clear!

el suyo, la suya, los suyos, las suyas each have several possible meanings: 'his', 'hers', 'theirs', 'yours' (polite), and occasionally their meaning may not be clear. To make things crystal clear you need to replace them with the following:

su casa → la suya → **la** de él/ella/usted/ellos/ellas/ustedes
sus casas → las suyas → **las** de él/ella/usted/ellos/ellas/ustedes
su hijo → el suyo → **el** de él/ella/usted/ellos/ellas/ustedes
sus hijos → los suyos → **los** de él/ella/usted/ellos/ellas/ustedes

el, **los**, **la**, **las**, agree in gender and number with the possessed thing, not with the person who possesses it.

Mental gymnastics 4

Replace the phrase with its equivalent.

Example: **su hijo (his)** → **el hijo de él**

1 su madre (hers) ....
2 sus zapatos (his) ....
3 su billete (yours, singular) ....
4 su médico (theirs = Julia and Claudia) ....
5 sus problemas (yours, plural) ....
6 sus perros (theirs = Pedro and Pablo) ....

How to say *I*, *you*, *he*, *she*, *it*, *we* and *they*

6

In English, 'I', 'you', 'he', 'she', 'it', 'we' and 'they' can help us understand what a sentence is about. When this is the case, they are called the **subject** (G). For example, in the sentence 'They visited some old friends on Sunday', 'they' is the subject of the sentence.

In this unit, you'll learn the Spanish equivalents for 'I', 'you', 'he', 'she', 'we', 'you', 'they' (when these words are the subject), and how to use them.

All these words are called **pronouns** (G) and pronouns are words that take the place of a noun: 'John has a fever'. 'He' is sick. In both of these sentences 'John' and 'he' are the subjects of the sentences – what the sentence is about – and 'he' is a subject pronoun that stands for 'John'.

I, he, she and it

Here are the equivalents of 'I', 'he', 'she' and 'it'.

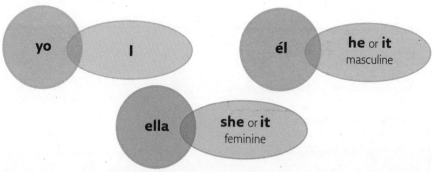

It
'It' may be translated as **él** or **ella** but in practice Spanish rarely uses **él** or **ella** when referring to things. Let's take an example: **la mesa** (the table). In English, to refer to the table you would use 'it': 'it is rectangular', 'it is expensive', etc. In Spanish, you just say: **es rectangular**, **es cara** (literally 'is rectangular', 'is expensive').

Five words for 'you'

There are five words for 'you' in Spanish. Here is how you choose which one to use:

tú   for people you know very well – your family, friends, colleagues, young people or children – and when you're talking to only **one person**.

vosotros   for if you are talking to a group of males or a mixed group
vosotras   if you are talking to a group of females.

usted   for when you are talking to **one person** with whom you need to be **formal**. Use **usted** when meeting an older stranger, a person in authority or an elderly person.

ustedes   for when you are talking politely or **formally** to **more than one person**

If you find yourself in a formal situation use **tú** only when invited to do so. People may tell you: **No me trates de usted** or **Por favor, tutéame.**

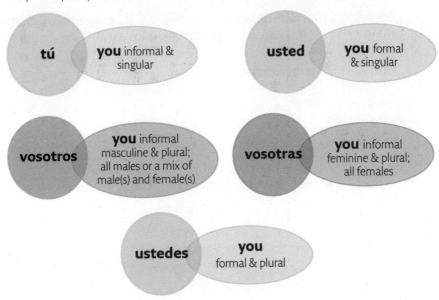

Two forms of 'we'

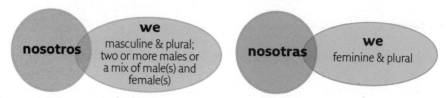

nosotros — **we** masculine & plural; two or more males or a mix of male(s) and female(s)

nosotras — **we** feminine & plural

Two words for 'they'

ellos — **they** masculine & plural; two or more males or a mix of male(s) and female(s)

ellas — **they** feminine & plural

Tony's Tip

If you remember **by looking at things**, write the words on a new piece of paper. Write with colours too!

If you remember better **with sounds**, link the words and their gender to **a rhythm or a melody** (a jingle or a rap); record yourself and listen regularly.

You could also **link each word with sounds**:

yo sounds like 'yo-yo'
tú sounds like 'too'
él sounds like the letter 'l'

If you remember better when doing something, **do some action** while memorising, e.g. **write the words on cards** and move the cards around. Doodle or play with a stress ball.

You could write or draw the words with their sounds. Remember **yo** by drawing it in a yo-yo, for example.

Mental gymnastics 1

Take two minutes to memorise as many words on the previous page as you can. Use the tips above and your own memory techniques.

How many words can you now remember without looking back?

Try to recall them again in **two hours**, in **one day**, in **one week**, in **one month** and in **six months**. The more you repeat them, the longer you will remember them.

Mental gymnastics 2

Find the Spanish equivalents of 'I', 'you' (informal singular), 'you' (informal feminine plural), 'he', 'she', 'we' (masculine), 'they' (feminine) in this grid.

N	L	É	E	S	Y	N	L
O	O	L	L	E	E	O	S
S	A	L	L	E	S	O	E
O	R	N	A	S	N	U	Y
T	Y	Y	L	E	O	L	K
R	U	L	N	Y	N	S	L
O	V	R	Y	O	O	A	O
S	A	R	T	O	S	O	V

Mental gymnastics 3

Solve the anagrams to find the Spanish equivalents of 'I', 'you' (formal), 'you' (informal), 'he', 'she', 'we' and 'they' (feminine).

1	LAELS	....	5	ÚT	....
2	ORSOTSON	....	6	SARVTOOS	....
3	LÉ	....	7	OY	....
4	UTDES	....	8	LELA	....

Mental gymnastics 4

Which word would you choose in the following situations?

yo • tú • usted • él • ella • nosotros • nosotras • vosotros • vosotras ustedes • ellos • ellas

1   To speak to the Spanish Prime Minister?...
2   To talk about your friends and yourself?...
3   To speak to your Spanish friend's child?...
4   To speak to your Spanish friend's children?......................................
5   To talk about your dog?..
6   To talk about your daughters? ....
7   To speak to the Spanish shop assistant you're meeting
    for the first time?..
8   To speak to your Spanish friend's parents for the first time?
    ....
9   To talk about your female boss?...
10 To talk about your parents-in-law? ....
11 To talk about your nephews?..
12 To talk about yourself?...

How to say *to be* using the verb *ser*

Ser

This is a **verb** (**G**). Its **basic form**, the one you find in a dictionary, is **ser** (to be). In English, verbs are normally preceded by 'I', 'you', 'he', etc.: 'I am', 'you are'. In Spanish these words aren't usually necessary, because the verb forms make clear who is doing the action.

Notice that the verb forms used with **usted** and **ustedes** are the ones used with **él/ella** and **ellos/ellas** respectively; this is true for all Spanish verbs.

Subject pronouns	ser (to be)	Pronunciation	Meaning
yo	**soy**	*so*y	I am
tú	**eres**	*e*-res	you are
usted; él/ella	**es**	es	you are; he/she/it is
nosotros/ nosotras	**somos**	*so*-mos	we are
vosotros/ vosotras	**sois**	*so*ees	you are
ustedes; ellos/ellas	**son**	son	you are; they are

Mental gymnastics 1

Take two minutes to memorise as many words from the table as you can.

How many words can you now recall without looking at the table?

Repeat and succeed!
To fix information in your long-term memory you should repeat it at fixed points after you first learnt it, following this formula:

1st repetition: an hour or so after
2nd repetition: a day after
3rd repetition: a week after
4th repetition: a month later
5th repetition: six months after

So in an hour's time, revise **ser**!

Mental gymnastics 2

Find the different forms of **ser** in the grid. Some of them are backwards.

```
O   S   O   M   O   S

E   E   Y   S   O   N

O   R   O   I   S   S

O   E   S   S   E   E

S   I   E   N   I   E

N   S   S   R   Y   S
```

Mental gymnastics 3

Complete the words with their missing vowels.

1   LLS SN ....
2   VSTRS SS ....
3   STD S ....
4   Y SY...
5   NSTRS SMS ....
6   T RS ....

Using ser

ser + adjective to describe people, animals and things.

ser is used to refer to physical appearance (e.g. shape, height, colour) personality traits, nationality:

Yo soy alto y simpático.	I am tall and friendly.
Nosotros somos españoles.	We are Spanish.
Las faldas son azules y cortas.	The skirts are blue and short.
Nuestro gato es bonito pero agresivo.	Our cat is pretty but aggressive.

ser + noun or pronoun to say what someone or something is:

Soy yo, Emilia.	It's me, Emilia.
Madrid es la capital de España.	Madrid is the capital of Spain.
Mi novio es abogado.	My boyfriend is *a lawyer.

*Spanish does not use the article when stating a person's occupation.

ser de to refer to where someone or something comes from:

Soy de Londres.	I'm from London.
Nuestra profesora es de Bilbao.	Our teacher is from Bilbao.

ser de to express possession:

El libro es de tu hermano.	It's your brother's book.
El dinero es *mío.	The money is mine.

*The article preceding the possessive pronoun is not normally necessary when it follows **ser**.

ser de to express what something is made of:

La mesa es de madera.	The table is made of wood.
La lámpara es de plástico.	The lamp is made of plastic.

ser para to indicate purpose or recipient:

El cuchillo es para cortar.	The knife is for cutting.
Esta televisión es para ti.	This television is for you.

To refer to the price of something:

¿Cuánto es?	How much is it?
Son 300 euros.	It's 300 euros.

To say what time it is and what day it is:

Es la una.	It's 1 o'clock.
Son las dos y cuarto de la tarde.	It's 2.15 in the afternoon.
Hoy es domingo.	It's Sunday today.

Mental gymnastics 4

Make sentences with **ser** linking the phrases in the left-hand column with those in the right-hand column.

1	Juan .....**es**.......	abogados.
2	Este zumo	aburrida y larga.
3	Sus tíos	australianos.
4	El salón	de Barcelona.
5	La cama	británica.
6	Mis perros	de madera.
7	Su jefa	de naranja.
8	Hoy	el café?
9	¿Cuánto	exigente.
10	Nosotros	grande y luminoso.
11	El reloj	hijas de Dolores?
12	La novela	lunes.
13	Yo	preciosos.
14	Vosotras, ¿	redondo.

Mental gymnastics 5

Read the text and rewrite it by changing the subject from **nosotros** (we) to **yo** (I). You decide if you want to write a feminine or a masculine version. Don't forget that other words will change as well as the verbs!

Nosotros somos españoles, somos de Málaga. Somos unas personas agradables, pacientes, optimistas y trabajadoras. No somos guapos, somos altos y delgados. Somos fotógrafos. Somos hijos de un pintor y una profesora y nietos de un arquitecto importante de Málaga. Nuestra casa es de madera y es antigua. Es grande y el salón es bonito y original.

Yo soy ....
....
....
....
....
....

Mental gymnastics 6

Write the following sentences in Spanish:

1   Jaime is from Chile. ....
2   The sofa is made of leather. ....
3   It is half past one. ....
4   Today is Wednesday. ....
5   They are boring. ....
6   We are not English, we are Scottish. ....
7   My mother is a nurse. ....
8   Samuel's friend is intelligent. ....
9   The money is for Carlos. ....
10 The knife is to cut the omelette. ....

How to say *to be* using the verb *estar*

8

In this unit you are going to learn the irregular verb **estar** and how to use it.

Estar

Subject pronouns	estar (to be)	Pronunciation	Meaning
yo	estoy	es**toy**	I am
tú	estás	es-**tas**	you are
usted; él/ella	está	es-**ta**	you are; he/she/it is
nosotros/ nosotras	estamos	es-**ta**-mos	we are
vosotros/ vosotras	estáis	es-**tais**	you are
ustedes; ellos/ellas	están	es-**tan**	you are; they are

This is a verb (**G**). Its <u>basic form</u>, the one you find in a dictionary, is **estar** (to be). In English, verbs are normally preceded by 'I', 'you', 'he', etc.: 'I am', 'you are'. In Spanish these words aren't usually necessary, because the verb forms make it clear who is doing the action.

Notice that the verb forms used with **usted** and **ustedes** are the ones used with **él/ella** and **ellos/ellas** respectively; this is true for <u>all</u> Spanish verbs.

Mental gymnastics 1

Take two minutes to memorise as many words on the previous page as you can.

How many words can you now recall without looking back at the previous page?

Mental gymnastics 2

Complete the words with their missing vowels.

1 L ST ....
2 STDS STN ....
3 VSTRS STS ....
4 Y STY ....
5 NSTRS STMS ....
6 T STS ....

Some uses of estar

- **estar + adjective** to describe the state or condition of people, animals and things:

Yo estoy cansado.	I am tired.
Nuestro coche está viejo.	Our car is old.
Tu perro está enfermo.	Your dog is sick.
El café está frío.	The coffee is cold.
El banco está cerrado.	The bank is closed.
La lavadora está rota.	The washing machine is broken.
Mi novia está contenta.	My girlfriend is happy.

- **estar** to talk about the location of people, animals and things:

Juan está en casa.	Juan is at home.
El libro está encima de la mesa.	The book is on the table.
El gato está debajo del sofá.	The cat is under the sofa.

- **estar** to express distance:
  Londres está a una hora de Oxford.   London is one hour from Oxford.
  Madrid está a 550 kilómetros de Santiago.   Madrid is 550 km from Santiago.
  Glasgow está cerca de Edimburgo.   Glasgow is near Edinburgh.
  Sidney está lejos de Perth.   Sydney is far from Perth.

- **estar** to talk about health:
  Mi hijo está mal, está enfermo.   My son is unwell, he is sick.
  Elena está bien.   Elena is well.

- **estar** is also used in some set phrases:
  estar de pie   to be standing
  estar de vacaciones   to be on holidays
  estar de viaje   to be travelling
  estar de moda   to be fashionable
  estar de buen/mal humor   to be in a good/bad mood

Mental gymnastics 3

Make sentences with **estar** linking the phrases in the left-hand column with those in the right-hand column.

1	Mis suegros están	cansados, trabajamos mucho.
2	Las llaves están	cerca de Liverpool.
3	Manchester está	cerrado los lunes.
4	Granada está a	contentos.
5	Tengo fiebre, estoy	de estar de pie.
6	Estamos	de moda.
7	El color rojo está	roto.
8	El museo está	de vacaciones en Cuba.
9	Mis hijos están	dos horas de mi casa.
10	El señor García no está,	en mi bolso.
11	Estoy cansado	enfermo.
12	El coche está	está de viaje.

Mental gymnastics 4

Write the following phrases in Spanish.

1   Is Laura on holidays? ....
2   The keys are on the table. ....
3   The cooker is broken. ....
4   The soup is very hot. ....
5   The boss is in a bad mood. ....
6   I'm in Barcelona. ....
7   My husband is on a trip. ....
8   The airport is near the train station. ....
9   My house is 20 km from the beach. ....
10   Holidays in Spain are fashionable. ....

Existence and location are not the same thing!

In English, to talk about the existence of people or things you can use the expressions 'there is' or 'there are':

There are many children.

Is there a bank near here?

In my city there are two hospitals.

In Spanish, you use the expression **hay** (*aee*):

Hay muchos niños.

¿Hay un banco cerca de aquí?

En mi ciudad hay dos hospitales.

hay is a special form of the Spanish verb **haber** and it is invariable, so it can refer without changing to the existence of one thing or several things. It never changes! The second example shows that it can be used in questions (is there?/are there?) as well as statements.

But if you want to talk about the location of people or things you already know about you must use **estar**.

Los niños están en el parque.	The children are in the park.
¿Dónde está el banco?	Where is the bank?
Los dos hospitales están en el centro.	The two hospitals are in the city centre.

How to talk about the present: regular verbs

9

The present tense

A **verb** (G) is a word, such as 'speak', 'eat' or 'live', which describes an action. When you are doing something now or if you do something regularly you might say '<u>he eats</u> paella', '<u>they listen</u> to music', '<u>I write</u> every day'. This is called the **present tense** (G – see Tense). It's not in the past or the future – it's in the present, it's now.

Endings and verbs types
Spanish verbs need you to add endings. Choosing an ending depends on **four** things:

1 what type of verb you're using
   Spanish verbs are classified according to the ending of their **infinitive** (G) (the name or basic form of the verb) and fall into three groups:
   - the –**AR** type
   - the –**ER** type
   - the –**IR** type

2 who or what is doing the action (the subject) (G), e.g. I, you, he, it, Marta …

3 when the action takes place (present, past or future) and
4 whether the verb is
   - **regular** (G – see Verb) (verbs that follow a predictable pattern) or
   - **irregular** (G – see Verb) (verbs, such as **ser** (to be) and **tener** (to have) do not follow normal rules)

Present tense of regular verbs: using the correct ending
To create the correct form of the verb in Spanish, first take off the ending that you have found in the dictionary:

habl<u>ar</u> → **habl**

com<u>er</u> → **com**

viv<u>ir</u> → **viv**

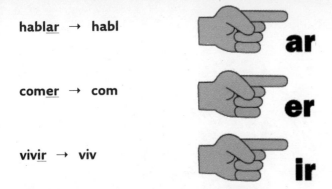

Then add the endings to the bit you are left with, which is called the stem (**G**):
habl
com
viv

Each **yo**, **tú**, **usted**, **el/ella**, **nosotros/nosotras**, **vosotros/vosotras**, **ustedes**, **ellos/ellas** calls for a specific ending.

For example, for **hablar** the ending for **yo** is **-o**
(yo) habl + **o** = **(yo) habl**o I live
and the ending for **tú** is **-as**
(tú) hablas you live

Supposing you wanted to say 'I speak Spanish' in Spanish:

→ you take **hablar**
→ then you take off the **-ar** bit

→ then you add the ending for **yo** (which is **-o**) to the stem:
→ **habl**-o
→ **habl**o
→ **habl**o **español**

In English verbs are normally preceded by 'I', 'you', 'he', 'she', etc.: 'I work', 'you eat', 'he lives'. In Spanish these words aren't usually necessary, because the verb endings make it clear who is doing the action. **hablo español** can only mean 'I speak Spanish': the ending **-o** tells us that the person who speaks Spanish is **yo**.

Let's look at each of these verb types.

1 the -AR type

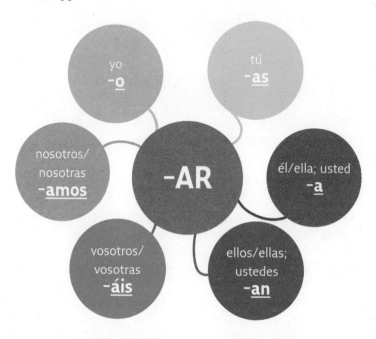

Did you notice? The verb ending used with **usted** and **ustedes** (the polite words for 'you' singular and plural) is the one used with **él/ella** and **ellos/ellas** respectively; this is true for <u>all</u> Spanish verbs.

Here are some useful **-AR** verbs:

alqui**lar**	to rent	desayu**nar**	to have breakfast
and**ar**	to walk	estudi**ar**	to study
apag**ar**	to switch off	escuch**ar**	to listen, hear
arreg**lar**	to arrange, set in order,	habl**ar**	to speak
	settle, repair, adjust	limpi**ar**	to clean
cen**ar**	to have dinner	pag**ar**	to pay
comp**rar**	to buy	traba**jar**	to work

Mental gymnastics 1

Take two minutes to memorise as many words on the previous page as you can. Use the Tony's tips and your own memory techniques.

How many endings can you now recall without looking back at the previous page?

Try to recall them again in **two hours**, in **one day**, in **one week**, in **one month** and in **six months**. The more you repeat them, the longer you will remember them.

Mental gymnastics 2

Complete the following verbs.

1   nosotros habl- *amos*
2   ustedes pag- *an*
3   él limpi- *a*
4   yo compr- *o*
5   vosotros alquil- *aís*
6   ellas trabaj- *an*
7   tú estudi- *as*
8   usted cen- *an*

2 the -ER type

Here are the endings
for the regular
-ER verbs:

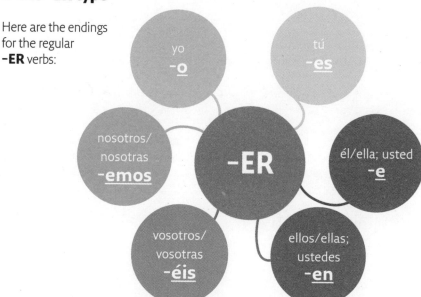

yo
-o

tú
-es

nosotros/
nosotras
-emos

-ER

él/ella; usted
-e

vosotros/
vosotras
-éis

ellos/ellas;
ustedes
-en

Here are some useful **-ER** verbs:

aprend**er**	to learn	met**er**	to insert, put in
beb**er**	to drink	pose**er**	to own, possess
com**er**	to eat	repond**er**	to reply
corr**er**	to run	tos**er**	to cough
le**er**	to read	vend**er**	to sell

Mental gymnastics 3

Complete the words with their missing vowels. Verbs to look for in different
forms: **aprender**, **beber**, **comer**, **leer**, **meter**, **responder**, **vender**.

1   TÚ MTS *metes*
2   NSTRS BBMS *bebemos*
3   YO CM *comer*
4   VSTRS LS *leéis*

5   STD VND *venden*
6   LLS PRNDN *ellos prenden*
7   LL RSPND *responde*

3 the -IR type

Here are the endings for the regular **-IR** verbs:

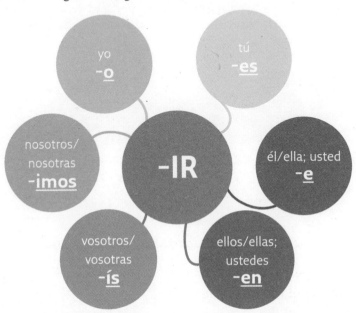

Here are some useful **-IR** verbs:

abr**ir**	to open
cumpl**ir**	to carry out, fulfil, reach (an age)
decid**ir**	to decide
discut**ir**	to discuss
divid**ir**	to divide
escrib**ir**	to write
sub**ir**	to rise, climb, go up, board
viv**ir**	to live

There is another way of talking about something you are doing <u>now</u> in English – 'I am walking', 'he is running', 'they are talking'. In Spanish, you can just use the normal present tense for this. For example 'I am working' is **trabajo**. 'We are eating' is **comemos**. Simple!

Mental gymnastics 4

Join the halves together to complete the verbs and add the correct subject (**yo**, **tú**, **ella**, **nosotros**, **vosotros** or **ustedes**). For some there are several possible correct answers.

-timos   -ides   -iden   -plo   -imos   -vís   -ribe   -res

1 ....   cum-................
2 ....   dec-................
3 ....   esc-................
4 ....   vi-................
5 ....   ab-................
6 ....   sub-................
7 ....   div-................
8 ....   discu-................

Tony's Tip

Find patterns and you will remember

Think of the regular verbs as the good guys, because these are the verbs that behave in a predictable manner.

- Each **-ar**, **-er**, **-ir** type verb has six forms and each form has a specific ending.
- The ending for **yo** is **-o** for all of them.
- The endings of the **-ar** type verbs always start with an **-a** (except for **yo**): **-as**, **-a**, **-amos** and so on.
- The endings of the **-er** type verbs always start with an **-e** (except for **yo**): **-es**, **-e**, **-emos** and so on.
- The endings for **tú**, **él/ella**, **usted**, **ellos/ellas**, **ustedes** of the **-ir** type verbs are the same as the **-er** type. Only the endings for **nosotros/nosotras** and **vosotros/vosotras** are different: **-imos**, **-ís**.

You can use the verb wheel that accompanies this book to practise the regular verbs.

Mental gymnastics 5

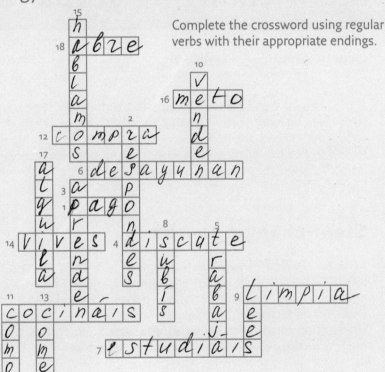

Complete the crossword using regular verbs with their appropriate endings.

Across

1 Yo ... la comida. (pagar)
4 (Ella) ... con Juan. (discutir)
6 (Ellos) ... cereales y fruta. (desayunar)
7 ¿(Vosotros) ... inglés? (estudiar)
9 Lola ... la cocina. (limpiar)
11 Vosotros ... bien. (cocinar)
12 (Usted) ... un coche. (comprar)
14 ¿(Tú) ... en Londres? (vivir)
16 Yo ... el coche en el garaje. (meter)
18 El banco ... a las nueve. (abrir)

Down

2 ¿(tú) ... al email? (responder)
3 Tus hijos ... español. (aprender)
5 Juan ... en Bilbao. (trabajar)
8 ¿(Vosotros) ...? (subir)
9 Tú ... mucho. (leer)
10 (Ellos) ... su casa. (vender)
11 (Yo) .... a las dos. (comer)
13 Pablo ... tortilla. (comer)
15 (Nosotros) ... chino. (hablar)
17 Elena ... un piso. (alquilar)

How to talk about the present: stem-changing verbs

10

In Spanish, there are a few **verbs** (G) belonging to a group whose **stem** (G) changes in some forms: these verbs are known as 'stem-changing' verbs.

In this unit you are going to study the **present tense** (G) of some common stem-changing verbs. Bear in mind that as there isn't a way of easily identifying verbs in this category, and since many of them are in everyday use, you will have to make the effort to learn them off by heart. However, once you understand how stem-changing verbs work it won't be too difficult to get the hang of them! Use the verb wheel that accompanies this book to learn them.

Stem-changing verbs

A number of verbs are **irregular** (G) in some of the forms of the stem. Remember, the stem is the bit you are left with after removing the **-ar**, **-er** or **-ir** ending of the basic form of a verb: **pensar** (to think) → **pens-**. The good news is that the endings of stem-changing verbs are the same as for regular verbs and that the stem change affects <u>all</u> the forms: **yo**, **tú**, **él/ella**, **usted**, **ellos/ellas**, **ustedes** <u>apart from</u> the **nosotros/nosotras** and **vosotros/vosotras** forms.

These verbs are grouped in three types:

- **Type 1:** e → ie
- **Type 2:** o → ue
- **Type 3:** e → i (only a few **-ir** verbs)

Let's see how it works. If, for example, you want to find out the forms of the verb **pensar** which belong to type 1: e → ie:

→ take off the **-ar** bit, so you are left with the stem:

pens-  **ar**

→ then you change the **e** of the stem to **ie** in <u>all</u> the forms <u>apart from</u> **nosotros** and **vosotros**

p**ie**ns-

→ finally you add the endings (**-o**, **-as**, **-a**, **-an**) to the stem:
→ (yo) p**ie**ns**o**, (tú) p**ie**ns**as**, (él/ella; usted) p**ie**ns**a**, (ellos/ellas; ustedes) p**ie**ns**an**

The **nosotros** and **vosotros** forms have a regular stem, so changes are not necessary; the only thing you have to do is to add the ending to the stem: **(nosotros/nosotras) pens**amos, **(vosotros/vosotras) pens**áis

Let's look at each of these verb types more closely.

Type 1: e → ie

Here are some useful **-e → -ie** verbs:

calentar	to heat
cerrar	to close
comenzar	to begin, to start
despertar	to wake
divertir	to entertain, amuse
encender	to switch on, to light
entender	to understand
fregar	to wash up
merendar	to have an afternoon snack
pensar	to think
perder	to lose
preferir	to prefer
querer	to want, to love
sentar	to sit
tener	to have

Note that the stem for **yo** is different in the verb **tener** (to have): **tengo, tienes, tiene, tenemos, tenéis, tienen**.

Mental gymnastics 1

Take two minutes to memorise as many words in the above list as you can. Use the tips above and your own memory techniques.

Remember: the stem change (-e → -ie) affects all forms apart from the **nosotros/nosotras** and **vosotros/vosotras** forms. The endings for all forms are the same as for the regular verbs.

How many forms can you now recall without looking back at the previous page?

Type 2: o → ue

Here are some useful **-o → -ue** verbs:

acostar(se)	to go to bed, to lay down	probar	to prove, to taste, to try on
almorzar	to lunch	recordar	to remember
costar	to cost	renovar	to renew
dormir	to sleep	soler	to be in the habit, to 'usually'
encontrar	to find	sonar	to sound
mostrar	to show	soñar	to dream
mover	to move	volar	to fly
poder	to be able, can	volver	to come back

Note that **jugar** (to play), with a stem vowel **u**, follows the same pattern as verbs with stem vowel **o**: **juego, juegas, juega, jugamos, jugáis, juegan**.

Mental gymnastics 2

Take two minutes to memorise as many words on the previous page as you can. Use the tips above and your own memory techniques.

Remember: the stem change (–o → –ue) affects all forms <u>apart from</u> the **nosotros/nosotras** and **vosotros/vosotras** forms. The endings for all forms are the same as for the regular verbs.

How many forms can you now recall without looking back at the previous page?

Type 3: e → i (only a few –ir verbs)

Here are some useful **-e** → **-i** verbs:

competir	to compete	pedir	to ask for
corregir	to correct	repetir	to repeat
elegir	to choose	seguir	to follow
impedir	to prevent	vestir	to dress
medir	to measure		

Note: corregir/elegir g → j before **o**:
corrijo, corriges, corrige, corregimos, corregís, corrigen
seguir gu → g before **o**:
sigo, sigues, sigue, seguimos, seguís, siguen

Find patterns and you will remember
Think of the stem verbs as the 'odd family' because some of the forms of these verbs
behave in a distinct manner – but take heart, you'll find patterns in the irregularity of
most of these verbs which will help you learn them:

- The stem change affects all the forms apart from the **nosotros/nosotras** and
  vosotros/vosotras forms.
- All the forms have the same endings as the regular verbs.
- The types are: Type 1: **e → ie**
  Type 2: **o → ue (jugar: u → ue)**
  Type 3: **e → i (g → j: corregir: (yo) corrijo, gu → g: seguir: sigo)**

Mental gymnastics 3

Take two minutes to memorise as many words in the above list as you
can. Use the tips above and your own memory techniques.

Remember: the stem change (**-e → -i**) affects all forms apart from the
nosotros/nosotras and **vosotros/vosotras** forms. The endings for all
forms are the same as for the regular verbs.

How many forms can you now recall without looking back at the
previous page?

Mental gymnastics 4

Join the halves together to complete the verbs and add the correct subject (**yo**, **tú**, **ella**, **nosotros**, **vosotros** or **ustedes**). For some there are several possible correct answers.

–éis   **–en**   **–o**   **–imos**   **–a**   **–as**

1 .... corrij–.....................
2 .... dorm–.....................
3 .... prefier–.....................
4 .... jueg–.....................
5 .... volv–.....................
6 .... cierr–.....................

Mental gymnastics 5

Complete the words with their missing vowels. Work out the subject, then look for the following verbs in different forms:

almorzar • cerrar • competir • elegir • encender • medir • probar • recordar

1 T NCNDS ....
2 NSTRS PRBMS ....
3 LLS LGN ....
4 Y MD ....
5 VSTRS RCRDS ....
6 STD LMRZ ....
7 T CMPTS ....
8 Y CRR ....

Mental gymnastics 6

Complete the crossword using verbs
with their appropriate endings.

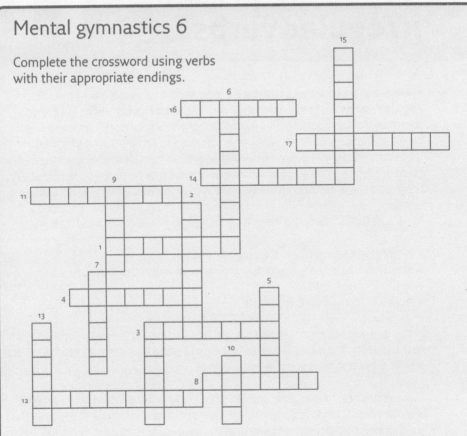

Across

1   Nosotras no ... al fútbol. (jugar)
3   Vosotras ... la comida. (probar)
4   Los pisos aquí ... mucho. (costar)
8   ¿... hambre (ustedes)? (tener)
11 ¿Qué ... (vosotros)? (preferir)
12 ¿(Tú) ... todo? (recordar)
14 Nosotros no ... como tú. (pensar)
16 El banco ... a las tres. (cerrar)
17 Mi familia ... a las dos. (almorzar)

Down

2   Yo ... a trabajar mañana. (comenzar)
3   Mi equipo de fútbol ...
    frecuentemente. (perder)
5   Ellas ... a su amiga. (vestir)
6   ¿Tú ...? (entender)
7   Mi hermana ... mañana. (volver)
9   ¡ ... yo! (elegir)
10 Yo ... (medir) 1.80.
13 Sara ... un coche nuevo. (querer)
15 (Nosotros) ... muchas horas. (dormir)

How to talk about the present: irregular verbs

There are a large number of **verbs** (G) in Spanish that do not follow the rules for **regular verbs** (G) as explained in Unit 9. These **irregular verbs** (G) are very common, so it's important that you try to learn how they work – for one thing, it's difficult to predict which group a verb belongs to just by looking at it! Check them on the verb wheel first, or in a dictionary and memorise them as you need them. It's worth making the effort to learn them off by heart as you're bound to come across the most common irregular verbs in conversation or when reading.

We are going to classify the irregular verbs in four groups to help you learn them:

- irregular verbs in the form corresponding to **yo**
- irregular verbs in the form corresponding to **yo** and in the stem
- totally irregular verbs
- stem-changing verbs (see unit 10)

In this unit you will learn some common irregular verbs in the first person singular (**yo**), some common irregular verbs in the first person singular and in the stem, as well as some totally irregular verbs.

In the verb wheel that accompanies this book, you will find lots of irregular verbs with the present tense endings nearest the rim of the wheel. Look at the wheel as you progress through this unit and use it for learning the irregular forms. We will try to find patterns to help you remember these slightly more difficult verbs.

Irregular verbs in the first person singular

A number of verbs are only irregular in the the form corresponding to **yo** of the present; the other forms: **tú**, **él**, **ella**, **usted** and so on, follow a regular pattern, i.e. they have regular endings. Let's take a look at them.

• Some verbs add g to the form corresponding to yo:

As with regular verbs, to create the correct form of the first person of the verb in Spanish, first take off the ending that you have found in the dictionary:

salir → sal  **ir**

Then add **g** to the bit you are left with, the **stem** (**G**):
salg

and then add the ending that corresponds to the first person of the present:
salg + **o** = (**yo**) **salgo** I go out

The forms for **tú**, **él/ella**, **usted**, **nosotros/nosotras**, **vosotros/vosotras**, **ellos/ellas**, **ustedes** follow a regular pattern.

So for the forms that correspond to **tú**, **él/ella** and so on, first take off the ending that you have found in the dictionary:

salir → sal  **er**

Then add the endings to the bit you are left with, the stem, which correspond to each form:

sal + **es**	= tú	**sales**	you go out
sal + **e**	= él/ella; usted	**sale**	he/she, you (polite) go out
sal + **imos**	= nosotros/nosotras	**salimos**	we go out
sal + **ís**	= vosotros/vosotras	**salís**	you go out
sal + **en**	= ellos/ellas; ustedes	**salen**	they, you (polite) go out

Some useful verbs that follow this pattern are: **poner** (to put) and its derivatives, e.g. **componer** (to compose), **imponer** (to impose), **exponer** (to expose), **proponer** (to propose) and **valer** (to be worth) and its derivatives, e.g. **equivaler** (to be equivalent/equal to).

● **hacer** (to do/to make) and its derivatives, e.g. **deshacer** (to undo/untie), **rehacer** (to redo/remake): **replace** the 'c' with 'g' in the form corresponding to **yo**. The other forms follow a regular pattern:
hago, **haces**, **hace**, **hacemos**, **hacéis**, **hacen**.

● Many verbs ending in **–acer** (except **hacer**), **–ecer**, **–ocer** and **–ucir** add 'z' to the form corresponding to **yo**.

conocer (to know): **conozco, conoces, conoce, conocemos, conocéis, conocen**
Other verbs: **agradecer** (to be grateful), **conducir** (to drive), **crecer** (to grow), **obedecer** (to obey), **ofrecer** (to offer) **producir** (to produce), **traducir** (to translate), **reconocer** (to recognise).

Have a look at **conducir** on the verb wheel.

● Verbs ending in **-uir**, such as **concluir** (to conclude), **construir** (to build), **contribuir** (to contribute), **distribuir** (to distribute), **incluir** (to include) place a **y** before the ending that does not begin with **i**. Thus the **nosotros** and **vosotros** forms remain unchanged.
construir: construyo, construyes, construye, construimos, construís, construyen.

Have a look at **incluir** on the verb wheel.

● **Other irregular verbs in the form corresponding to** yo **are:**
dar (to give): **doy**, das, da, damos, dais, dan
saber (to know): **sé**, sabes, sabe, sabemos, sabéis, saben
ver (to see, to watch): **veo**, ves, ve, vemos, veis, ven

Mental gymnastics 1

Join the halves together to complete the first person singular (**yo**) irregular form of the following verbs.

-oy   -o   -yo   -zco   -lgo   -ezco   -é   -yo   -co   -go

1	distribu-...................	6	traduz-.........................
2	cono-...........................	7	ha-...............................
3	sa-...............................	8	d-.................................
4	ve-...............................	9	agrad-.........................
5	s-................................	10	constru-......................

Mental gymnastics 2

Write the forms for **tú** and **nosotros** for the following verbs.

	tú	nosotros
decir		
saber		
ver		
salir		

Mental gymnastics 3

Write the forms for **él** and **vosotros** for the following verbs.

	él	vosotros
traducir		
hacer		
decir		
conocer		

Mental gymnastics 4

Complete the paragraph with the correct form of the verb in brackets.

Kate y Luke no .... (conocer) España pero................... (saber)
español. Ellos .... (ver) mucho la televisión española y
.... (traducir) del inglés al español. Además, frecuentemente,
.... (salir) con amigos españoles.

Irregular verbs in the form corresponding to yo and in the stem

Some verbs are irregular in the form corresponding to **yo** and in the stem but all of them have regular endings:

decir (to say, to tell): d**ig**o, d**i**ces, d**i**ce, decimos, decís, d**i**cen
oír (to hear): o**ig**o, o**y**es, o**y**e, oímos, oís, o**y**en
tener (to have): ten**g**o, t**ie**nes, t**ie**ne, tenemos, tenéis, t**ie**nen
venir (to come): ven**g**o, v**ie**nes, v**ie**ne, venimos, venís, v**ie**nen

Mental gymnastics 5

Solve these anagrams to find some more irregular verbs.

1   OY OGOI   ....
2   SOOTORSV CÍDSE   ....
3   LLESO INNEEV   ....
4   SUETD NITEE   ....
5   SROOOTSN IDSOECM ....
6   LALE EOY   ....
7   OY OIGD   ....
8   LÉ ENVEI   ....

Totally irregular verbs

These are verbs that do not follow a pattern. The main ones are: **haber** (to have), **ir** (to go), **ser** (to be), **estar** (to be). Have a look at them on the verb wheel.

Mental gymnastics 6

Complete the words with their missing vowels. Words to look for in different forms: **haber**, **ir**, **ser** and **estar**

1   T RS   ....
2   NSTRS HMS ....
3   LLS STN ....
4   Y H   ....
5   VSTRS SS ....
6   Y STY   ....
7   T VS   ....
8   Y SY   ....

Mental gymnastics 7

What do these sentences mean in English?

1   Hago mucho deporte. ....
2   Ella sabe hacer tortilla española. ....
3   Nosotros no conocemos a tu padre. ....
4   Juan traduce muy bien. ....
5   ¿Sabéis bailar salsa? ....
6   Vamos a Madrid mañana. ....
7   Salgo de casa a las ocho. ....
8   Tengo calor. ....

Mental gymnastics 8

Complete the crossword using irregular verbs with their appropriate endings.

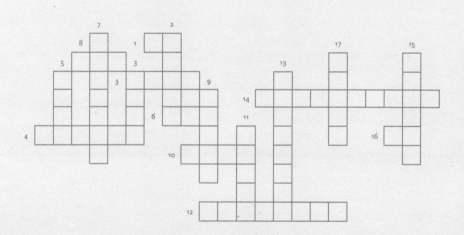

Across

1 Eva ... muy guapa. (ser)
3 La mesa no ... mucho. (valer)
4 ¿(Vosotros) ... frío? (tener)
6 Juan no ... bien. (oír)
8 Yo ... a tu casa por la tarde. (ir)
10 Yo ... la verdad. (decir)
12 Ustedes ... una solución. (proponer)
14 Mis tíos ... casas. (construir)
16 (Yo) no ... nadar. (saber)

Down

2 Yo ... mucho. (salir)
3 ¿(Vosotros) ... a Nueva Zelanda? (ir)
5 Ella ... unas fotos maravillosas. (hacer)
7 ¿(Tú) ... a Pedro? (conocer)
9 ¿(Vosotros) ... al cine? (venir)
11 Yo ... la mesa (poner)
13 Yo ... muy mal. (conducir)
15 Los niños ... hambre. (tener)
17 Ellas ... en casa. (estar)

Find patterns and you will remember

Think of the irregular verbs as the 'bad guys' because these are verbs which behave in a less predictable manner – but take heart, you'll find patterns in the irregularity of most of these verbs which will help you learn them:

- Irregular, but only in the stem of the form corresponding to **yo**. All the forms, including **yo**, have the same endings as the regular verbs: **salir**, **hacer**, **conocer**, **construir**, **dar**, **saber** and **ver**. Memorise the **yo** form and then make the other forms like any regular verb.
- Irregular in the the stem of the form corresponding to **yo** and in all the others except **nosotros** and **vosotros**. All the forms, including **yo**, have the same endings as the regular verbs: **decir**, **oír**, **tener**, **venir**. This type of verbs requires a bigger effort: the secret to remembering them lies in the old adage 'practice makes perfect'.
- Totally irregular verbs: different forms for each person (**yo**, **tú**, **él/ella**, **usted** and so on): **haber**, **ir**, **ser** and **estar**. Memorise them and link their forms to a song or images of your own creation to help you remember them.

Tony's Tip

How to remember your verbs

If you learn well by hearing, you could make up some songs of your own and use some verbs in the lyrics. Which English word(s) do the Spanish verbs and forms sound like? Alternatively you can make your own associations. The more personal or crazier, the better you'll remember the verbs!

You could also write or record a personal profile using the irregular verbs: **hago deporte**, **veo la televisión**, **no conduzco**, etc.

Little and often: you could set yourself a goal of learning (say) two irregular verbs a day or a week.

Commuting wheel: use the verb wheel anywhere to learn them: e.g. on the bus, during your lunch break or in the park.

Remember 'no pain, no gain': learning the irregulars can seem a bit boring, but knowing them will get you beyond the basic set sentences and will enable you to say things you want to say for yourself in Spanish.

Mind Map it! Complete the following Mind Map to remember what you have learned about Spanish verbs in the last five units.

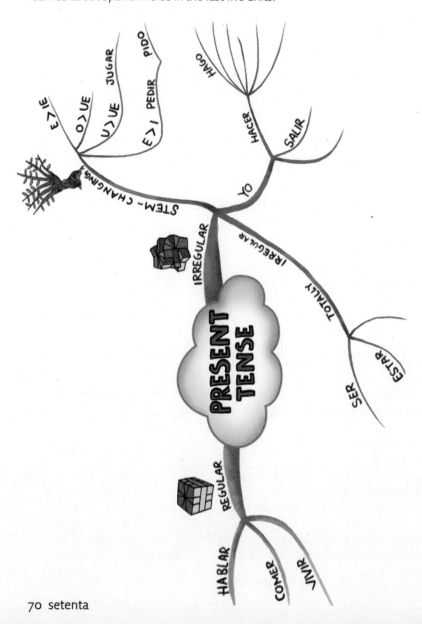

How to say *this*, *that*, *these* and *those*

12

In this unit you'll learn how to use words such as **this**, **that**, **these** and **those** to point to a particular object, animal or person.

This, that, these and those

This, **that**, **these** and **those** are called **demonstratives**. These words are used to point out a particular thing, animal or person, indicating their relative proximity to the speaker, either in space or in time. These words allow us to:

- select somebody or something from a group: **esta** fotografía (this photograph)
- refer to a specific place or time: **aquella** playa (that beach), **ese** verano (that summer).

This, that, these and those are determined by number only but their Spanish equivalents are determined by both gender and number.

	Masculine	**Feminine**	**Meaning**
Singular	este ese aquel	esta esa aquella	this (near to the speaker) that (near to the listener) that (further away from the speaker and the listener)
Plural	estos esos aquellos	estas esas aquellas	these (near to the speaker) those (near to the listener) those (further away from the speaker and the listener)

When you want to say 'this/these' or 'that/those' in Spanish, you need to think about the relative distance between the people having a conversation and the people or objects they are talking about. The pictures on page 72 should help you work out which word to use.

aquella

esa

esta

Spanish, like English, distinguishes between **demonstrative adjectives** (G) and **demonstrative pronouns** (G). They share the same form in the masculine and feminine, singular and plural.

- **Demonstrative adjectives** are used with a noun to point out a particular thing or person. As in English, Spanish demonstrative adjectives go before the noun.

- **este**, **ese**, **aquel** are used before a masculine singular noun and **esta**, **esa**, **aquella** are used before a feminine singular noun.
- **estos**, **esas**, **aquellos** are used before a masculine plural noun and **estas**, **esas**, **aquellas** are used before a feminine plural noun.

este niño	this boy	**estas sillas**	these chairs
esos pisos	those flats	**esa profesora**	that female teacher
aquel sombrero	that hat (over there)	**aquella gata**	that female cat (over there)

Golden rule

Demonstrative adjectives agree in gender and number with the noun to which they refer:

Demonstrative pronouns are used instead of a noun to point out people or things. They too agree in gender and number with the noun to which they refer.

Quiero **ese** sombrero. I want that hat.
¿Cuál, **este**? Which one, this one?
No, **aquel**. No, that one, over there.

Quiero **esa** camisa. I want that shirt.
¿Cuál, **esta**? Which one, this one?
No, **aquella**. No, that one, over there.

In the above examples, the masculine singular pronouns **este** and **aquel** refer to **sombrero**, a masculine singular noun; the feminine singular pronouns **esta** and **aquella** refer to **camisa**, a feminine singular noun.

How to say 'this or that thing'

To talk about unspecified objects, or to express a general idea or statement, use the demonstrative pronouns **esto**, **eso**, **aquello**. Their forms are invariable. They don't have a gender.

¿Puedes mandarle **esto** a Juan?
¿Y **eso** qué es?
Eso es todo.
Aquello es mío.

Could you send this to Juan?
And what's that?
That's it. That's all.
That (over there) is mine.

Mental gymnastics 1

How would you say the following in Spanish?

1   That's good. ....
2   I don't understand this. ....
3   What is that over there? ....
4   Do you understand that? ....
5   This is terrible! ....

Mental gymnastics 2

Complete the phrases with the appropriate demonstrative. Remember to match up the demonstrative with the noun to which it refers in terms of gender and number.

Use 'this/these':

1 .... sofá   2 .... ordenador   3 Quiero ....

Use 'that/those':

4 .... amigos   5 Quiero ....   6 .... jersey

Use 'that/those over there':

7 .... gafas de sol 8 .... limones   9 Quiero ....

Mental gymnastics 3

This quiz will show how well you know the Spanish equivalents for **this**, **that**, **these** and **those**. Choose the correct option for each sentence.

1 I prefer this one (about a car; un coche). **Prefiero ...**
   a   este
   b   estas
   c   ese

2 This novel is difficult. **... novela es difícil.**
   a   Esa
   b   Esta
   c   Aquel

3 I work in that hotel. **Trabajo en ... hotel.**
   a   aquel
   b   esa
   c   ese

4 I want those ones over there (about some shoes). **Quiero ...**
   a   aquel
   b   aquellos
   c   estos

5 These tables are too big **... mesas son demasiado grandes.**
   a   Esta
   b   Estas
   c   Este

6 We prefer these ones (about some boots). **Preferimos ...**
   a   estos
   b   esas
   c   estas

7 These ones are Spanish (speaking about cheeses). **... son españoles.**
   a Este
   b Estas
   c Estos

8 That house over there is my father's house. **... casa es la casa de mi padre.**
   a Esa
   b Aquella
   c Esta

9 That woman is my boss. **... mujer es mi jefa.**
   a Ese
   b Esta
   c Esa

10 Those children over there are my sons **... son mis hijos.**
   a Estos
   b Aquellos
   c Aquellas

Mental gymnastics 4

Complete each sentence with the correct demonstrative from the list below:

aquél aquellas aquello ésas ese esta este esto estos estos

1 No quiero eso ni esto, quiero ....
2 .... estudiantes son inteligentes.
3 No quiero .... sombrero, quiero éste.
4 .... casas son muy caras.
5 .... coche es de mi hermano.
6 .... playa es maravillosa.
7 .... problemas son difíciles.
8 .... es interesante.
9 ¿Cuál quieres: este, ese o ....?
10 Esas son feas, ... son bonitas pero aquellas son horribles.

How to ask questions

In Spanish, there are a variety of ways of forming a question.

¿Sí o no?

In Spanish, there are two ways you can choose from to ask a question if the answer is likely to begin with 'yes' or 'no':

1 Make your voice go up!
You don't make any changes to a normal sentence, such as '**Vives en Nueva York.**' – just raise your voice at the end when you say it and put the question marks (¿?) at the beginning and the end of the sentence if you are writing it down.

¿Vives en Nueva York? Do you live in New York?

¿Trabajáis en Gran Bretaña? Do you work in Great Britain?

¿James y Sarah son australianos? Are James and Sarah Australian?

¿Está cansada? Is she tired?

2 Change the word order
When the subject (**G**) of the verb is mentioned, another way of asking questions is to change the word order so you put the verb (**G**) before the subject:
Juan está en casa → **¿Está Juan en casa?** Is Juan at home?

¿Compra mamá la comida? Is mum buying some food?
¿Trabaja Juan en Estados Unidos? Does Juan work in the United States?
¿Viene Lola mañana? Is Lola coming tomorrow?
¿Están tus padres en casa? Are your parents home?

3 Negative questions

To make a negative question just put **no** before the verb.

¿**No estás** cansada? Aren't you tired?

¿**No compra mamá** la comida? Isn't mum buying some food?

Mental gymnastics 1

The first time you meet some Spanish people they might have some questions about you and vice versa. Let's practise by turning these sentences into questions. Think about whether you could change the order of the words to make the question.

1	Usted es inglés.	....
2	Usted vive en Londres.	....
3	Eres estudiante.	....
4	No trabajas.	....
5	Usted está de vacaciones.	....
6	No quieres tomar algo.	....
7	Vives aquí.	....
8	Usted habla español.	....

Answering questions

To answer a question to which the answer is likely to be 'yes' or 'no', just use **sí** or **no**.

¿Quieres café?   ¿Vienes al cine?

Sí (por favor)/**No** (gracias)   **Sí/No**

But if **sí** or **no** is followed by a verb and the answer is negative, you have to say **no** twice.

¿Estás casado?

No, **no** estoy casado.

There is no rule as to when you should use either of the above options – just choose the way you prefer!

Mental gymnastics 2

Use the familiar words for 'you' (**tú/vosotros**) to make suitable questions for these answers.

1 Sí, vivo en Londres. ....
2 No, nosotros no tenemos hijos. ....
3 Sí, vivo en un piso con mi novia. ....
4 Sí, mi familia vive en Nueva Zelanda. ....
5 No, estoy divorciado. ....
6 Sí, trabajo en Manchester. ....

Any other questions?

You can ask questions by using question words:

Things to remember

<u>All</u> the question words always have an accent when written down. Watch out for the difference between **por qué** (meaning **why**) and **porque** (which means **because**). Use **quién** when asking about one person and **quiénes** when asking about more than one person:

¿Quién llama? Who is calling?
¿Quiénes son? Who are they?

To make questions with a question word you need the following elements:
a question word + verb + subject

Julia trabaja → **¿Dónde trabaja Julia?**

Question words and prepositions

In Spanish, as in English, a question word may appear with a preposition but remember that the preposition always goes before the question word and <u>never</u> at the end of a question:

¿De dónde eres? Where do you come from?
¿Con quién sales? Who are you going out with?
(Literally 'With whom are you going out?')

Mental gymnastics 3

Solve these anagrams to find the question words.

1 ULÁC   ....
2 PRO UQÉ   ....
3 UDCOÁN   ....
4 ÉUQ   ....
5 CÓOM   ....
6 NDDÓE   ....
7 CLSUEÁ   ....
8 CTNUOÁ   ....
9 DAENDÓ   ....

Mental gymnastics 4

Rearrange the words to make a question.

1   ¿de eres dónde?   ....
2   ¿esta vas adónde tarde?   ....
3   ¿cuántos tienes hijos?   ....
4   ¿al vas por aeropuerto qué?   ....
5   ¿es cuánto?   ....
6   ¿tus vienen amigos cuándo?   ....
7   ¿estudias qué idiomas?   ....
8   ¿cómo novio es tu?   ....

Which question word to use?

1 **qué**, **cuál** or **cuáles** can be used to mean **which** and they convey the idea of selection.

• **¿Qué + noun?**
¿ **Qué** camisa quieres? Which shirt do you want?
¿ **Qué** actores prefieres? Which actors do you prefer?

• **¿Cuál** (which one?)/**Cuáles** (which ones?) + **verb?**

These words are used to mean **which** when there is a choice between two or more things.
¿ **Cuál** quieres? Which (one) do you want?
¿ **Cuáles** prefieres? Which (ones) do you prefer?

2 **¿Cuánto/Cuánta?** (How much?), **¿Cuántos/Cuántas?** (How many?)

Use **¿Cuánto/Cuánta?** (How much?), **¿Cuántos/Cuántas?** (How many?) to ask questions about quantity. There are four different words meaning 'how much?' and 'how many?' depending on whether the following word is masculine, feminine, plural or singular.

¿**Cuánto** dinero tienes? How much money do you have?
¿**Cuántos** hijos tienes? How many children do you have?
¿**Cuánta** leche quieres? How much milk do you want?
¿**Cuántas** cervezas quieres? How many beers do you want?

Mental gymnastics 5

Which one? Complete the following questions with **qué**, **cuál** or **cuáles**.

1   ¿........................ color prefieres?
2   ¿........................ deseas? ¿Este o ese?
3   ¿........................ ciudad está en la costa?
4   ¿........................ son tus ciudades preferidas?
5   ¿........................ es tu libro favorito?

Mental gymnastics 6

Complete the following questions with the appropriate question word.

1   ¿........................ periódicos lees?
2   ¿........................ agua bebes?
3   ¿........................ amigas españolas tienes?
4   ¿........................ aceite quieres?
5   ¿........................ idiomas hablas?

Question tags

In English, we often add tags such as 'isn't it?' 'don't you?' or 'haven't we?' to
questions where we anticipate a 'yes' or 'no' answer. In Spanish you can simply add
¿verdad? (literally 'truth?') to add a tag to your question.

Vienes al cine, **¿verdad?**   You're coming to the cinema, **aren't you**?
Quieres comer, **¿verdad?**   You want to eat, **don't you**?
Su novio es canadiense, **¿verdad?**   Her boyfriend is Canadian, **isn't he**?

Mental gymnastics 7

Match the questions with their answers.

1. ¿Vienes al cine esta tarde?

a. El rojo.

2. Tienes hijos, ¿verdad?

b. ¡Sí!

3. ¿Qué color prefieres?

c. Soy de Canadá.

4. ¿A qué hora vamos al cine?

d. Sí, tengo tres.

5. ¿De dónde eres?

e. A las seis.

Tony's Tip

You could write or record useful phrases for when you are on holiday in a Spanish-speaking country, e.g. **¿Dónde están los servicios?**, **¿A qué hora sale el tren?**

Mind Map it! Complete the questions Mind Map or do your own, using colours and adding some examples.

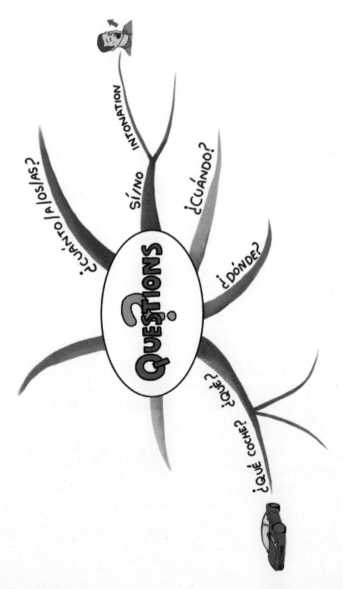

14

The reflexive family

Do it yourself

Some of the **regular** (G) and **irregular verbs** (G) can sometimes become **reflexive** (G), which means that the action is directed back to the person doing it – just as your **reflection** is directed back to you in a mirror.

In English, reflexive verbs look like this:

I wash **myself**
He shaves **himself**
We get (**ourselves**) **up**
The children get **dressed** (**themselves**)

They are more common in Spanish than in English. In Spanish you don't just say 'I brush my teeth' you say 'I myself brush my teeth'.

Reflexive Spanish

In Spanish, you add a reflexive bit, like in English you add 'myself'. You add it <u>before</u> the verb.

For example:
Yo **me lavo** los dientes   I brush my teeth
Yo **me despierto**   I wake (myself) up

The reflexive bits

There is one for each **subject** (G): **yo, tú, él/ella, usted, nosotros/ nosotras, vosotros/vosotras, ellos/ellas, ustedes.** They look like this:

me   myself
te   yourself (singular and informal)
se   himself/herself/itself; yourself (formal)

nos	ourselves
os	yourselves (informal)
se	themselves; yourselves (formal)

What to do with the reflexive bit?

This is when you may think you are starting to speak like a child proud of his or her independence: 'Look mum – I can wash myself! I can dress myself!'

You put the reflexive bits just <u>before</u> the verb. The order of words differs from English: it's like saying 'I myself wash'.

yo **me lavo**	I wash myself
tú **te lavas**	you wash yourself
él/ella; usted **se lava**	he/she washes himself/herself; you wash yourself
nosotros/nosotras **nos lavamos**	we wash ourselves
vosotros/vosotras **os laváis**	you wash yourselves
ellos/ellas; ustedes **se lavan**	they wash themselves; you wash yourselves

Dictionary listings

Verbs are normally listed under their **infinitive** (G) in the dictionary. You'll find out that a verb can be used as a reflexive with this little indication: (**se**), which is the reflexive bit that goes with the infinitive, e.g. acostar**se**.

Some useful reflexives for talking about your daily routine

despertar(**se**): e → ie	to wake up
levantar(**se**)	to get up (literally: to lift yourself up)
lavar(**se**)	to wash oneself
duchar(**se**)	to have a shower
maquillar(**se**)	to put on make up
afeitar(**se**)	to shave oneself
vestir(**se**): i → ie	to get dressed
peinar(**se**)	to comb one's hair
desvestir(**se**): e → i	to get undressed
acostar(**se**): o → ue	to go to bed

Have a look on the verb wheel at **despertarse, levantarse, vestirse** and **acostarse**.

Some useful reflexives to talk about accidents and injuries

romper(se)   to break
cortar(se)   to cut yourself
quemar(se)   to burn yourself
torcer(se)   to twist (e.g. your ankle)

A reflexive nuance

In Spanish, some of these verbs have two nuances: one in which the action is applied to myself, yourself, himself, etc.; another where the action is applied to someone or something else.

Let's look at some examples to see the differences in meaning.

Mi marido despierta a los niños todas las mañanas.
My husband wakes the children up every morning.
(Yo) me despierto todas las mañanas a las seis.
I wake up every morning at six.

(Yo) lavo el coche.
I wash the car.
(Yo) me lavo.
I wash (myself).

(Yo) levanto la silla.
I lift the chair.
(Yo) me levanto pronto.
I get up early.

Every time the action is turned back to **yo**, a **me** appears. It's the reflexive bit for **yo**.

Mental gymnastics 1

Match the pictures with the sentences.

a

b

c

d

e

f

1   Ella se maquilla.
2   Me ducho.
3   Él se afeita.
4   Ellas se peinan.
5   Nos vestimos.
6   Te acuestas.
7   Ellos se despiertan.
8   Te levantas.

g

h

Mental gymnastics 2

Rearrange the words in each question to make a phrase that includes a reflexive verb.

1   se – peina – María   ....
2   tú – vistes – te   ....
3   os – maquilláis – vosotros   ....
4   Juan y Pedro – afeitan – se ....
5   me – acuesto – yo   ....
6   nosotros – lavamos – nos   ....

Mental gymnastics 3

Write the correct form of the verb in brackets. Think about whether the action is applied to the subject or to someone (or something) else.

1   Yo .... a las diez de la noche. (acostar/acostarse)
2   La mujer .... al niño. (vestir/vestirse)
3   Pablo .... a Juan. (afeitar/afeitarse)
4   Nosotros .... la mesa. (levantar/levantarse)
5   ¿Vosotros .... a las siete? (levantar/levantarse)
6   La madre .... al bebé. (acostar/acostarse)

How to form negative statements

15

In English, to make something **negative**, you add **not**, **don't** or **doesn't**.

I am Spanish → I am **not** Spanish!
I work → I **don't** work.
Julia has children → Julia **doesn't** have any children.

No

In Spanish, to make something negative, you simply add **no** before the verb.

I am **not** Spanish!	¡**No** **soy** español!
I **don't** work.	**No trabajo**.
Julia **doesn't** have any children.	Julia **no** **tiene** hijos.

What about the reflexives with 'no'?
Remember the verbs used for describing your daily routine from Unit 14, such as **lavarse**: Yo me lavo (I wash)?

They follow a strict order:

1 (**yo, tú, él/ella, usted, nosotros/nosotras, vosotros/vosotras, ellos/ellas, ustedes**) or any **noun** (G)
    2 **no**
       3 **me, te, se, nos, os, se**
        4 **verb**

(Yo) **no me lavo**.	I don't wash.
Juan **no se afeita**.	Juan doesn't shave.

Mental gymnastics 1

Rearrange the words in each question to make a negative sentence.

1   hablamos – no – nosotros – español

    ....

2   nuestra – grande – casa – no – es

    ....

3   está – el – no – solucionado – problema

    ....

4   hambre – no – ellos – tienen

    ....

5   peino – me – yo – no – bien

    ....

6   tienen – los – no – frío – niños

    ....

7   quiero – no – visitar – el – museo

    ....

8   tenemos – no – euros

    ....

9   nos – no – vestimos – rápido

    ....

10   la – no – comida – hago

    ....

Affirmative and negative words

In English, words such as 'always', 'somebody', 'everybody' and 'anybody' are **affirmative** words (i.e the opposite of negative). All these words have a negative counterpart (e.g. never, nobody) so you can form negatives using them. The same type of words exists in Spanish. Let's look at some of the most common ones:

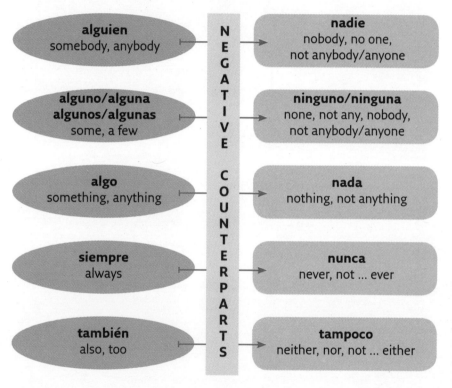

alguien somebody, anybody	→	**nadie** nobody, no one, not anybody/anyone
alguno/alguna algunos/algunas some, a few	→	**ninguno/ninguna** none, not any, nobody, not anybody/anyone
algo something, anything	→	**nada** nothing, not anything
siempre always	→	**nunca** never, not ... ever
también also, too	→	**tampoco** neither, nor, not ... either

NEGATIVE COUNTERPARTS

Negatives

All the previous negative words you have just learnt can form negative sentences as follows:

1 Placing no before the verb and the negative word after the verb

2 Placing the negative word before the verb

- **Ninguno** 'nobody', 'none', 'not anybody' may be used as an **adjective** (G) or a **pronoun** (G).
  1 As an adjective, **ninguno** agrees in **gender** (G) and number with the noun.
    Ninguno shortens to **ningún** before a masculine singular noun.
      No tengo **ningún** problema. I haven't got a problem (literally 'any problem').
      Sofía no quiere **ninguna** bebida. Sofía doesn't want a drink (lit. 'any drink').

  2 As a pronoun **ninguno** agrees in gender and number with the noun it replaces.
      No tengo **ninguno**. I haven't got any.
      Sofía no quiere **ninguna**. Sofía doesn't want any.
  Ninguno, ninguna is often followed by **nosotros/nosotras, vosotros/ vosotras, ellos/ellas, ustedes** or a noun.
      Ninguno de **vosotros** tiene coche. None of you have a car.
      No viene **ninguno** de **mis amigos**. None of my friends are coming.
  Take care with the verb form here: the Spanish verbs are singular in both of the above examples.

Notice that **algunos/algunas** – both <u>plural words</u> – have **ninguno/ninguna** – both <u>singular words</u> as a negative counterpart:

Tengo **algunos** libros. I have some books.
No tengo **ningún** libro. I haven't got any books.

● **Nadie** and **nada** are invariable pronouns. **Nadie** refers to people and **nada** to things without specifying which type of person or thing we are talking about:

No veo a **nadie**. I don't see anybody.
No veo **nada**. I don't see anything.

Sometimes negative words can be combined with each other. The first negative word goes before the verb and the second one goes after the verb.

Nunca hago **nada**. I never do anything.
Nunca viene **nadie**. No one ever comes.
Nadie quiere **nada**. No one wants anything.

Although double negatives are incorrect in standard English (e.g. 'he never does nothing around the house' should be 'he never does anything'), pairing negative words as in the above examples is grammatically correct in Spanish.

Mental gymnastics 2

Rewrite each sentence using two negative words.

Example: **Nunca salgo**   **No salgo nunca**

1   Nunca bebo. ....
2   Nada está en su sitio. ....
3   Nadie habla. ....
4   Tampoco quiero café. ....
5   Ninguno de los estudiantes está enfermo. ....
6   Ninguna persona hace deporte. ....
7   Nadie sabe latín. ....

Mental gymnastics 3

The interpreter got it all wrong: change these sentences to make them negative. Use two negative words.

Example: **Emilia siempre trabaja los viernes.**
Emilia no trabaja nunca los viernes.

1   Mi madre siempre come a la una. ....

....

2   Alguien entra. ....

3   Quiero algo para el dolor de cabeza. ....

....

4   Alguna de mis amigas habla inglés. ....

....

5   Tenemos algo. ....

6   Algunos quieren tortilla. ....

7   Siempre salgo los viernes. ....

8   Hoy vienen algunos amigos a cenar. ....

....

Tony's Tip

You could write or record some information about yourself that you might want to say during a holiday in a Spanish-speaking country. You could talk about things you don't have, activities you don't do (always useful if you have to decline unwelcome invitations) and who you are not, e.g. **No tengo tu número de teléfono**; **No juego al rugby**; **No soy australiana.**

How to compare people, things and actions 16

In this unit, you'll learn how to make comparisons.

More or less spacious than

In English, there are two ways to compare people or things. Either you add **-er** at the end of an **adjective** (G) or an **adverb** (G), e.g. **nice → nicer**, **fast → faster**, or you just use 'more' or 'less', e.g. **spacious → more/less spacious**, **more/less slowly**. Which of these two you use generally depends on the length of the word. If you want to introduce the person or thing you are making the comparison with, you add 'than'.

'More ... than' is más ... que

In Spanish, you use **más** followed by an adjective, adverb or noun (G) to make a comparison. The structure works like this:

Comparative adjectives agree in gender and number with the noun they describe.

Yo soy **más** alt**o** **que** mi hermano. (male speaking)	I'm **taller than** my brother.
Ella es **más** alt**a** **que** tú.	She's **taller than** you (are).
Tú juegas **más** despacio **que** Juan.	You play **more** slowly **than** Juan (does).
Mi padre tiene **más** hermanos **que** el tuyo.	My father has **more** brothers **than** yours (does).

Here's a variation for when you're comparing how actions are done.

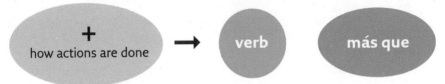

Los británicos **desayunan** más que los españoles.
The British eat **more** for breakfast **than** the Spanish.

'Less ... than' is menos ... que

To say something is 'less expensive' or 'less fast' (or say 'fewer brothers') you use the word **menos**:

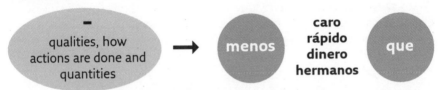

Golden rule

Comparative adjectives agree in gender and number with the noun they describe.

Yo soy **menos** alt**o** que mi hermano.
I'm **less** tall **than** my brother. (male speaking)
Ella es **menos** alt**a** que tú.   She's **less** tall **than** you.
Tú juegas **menos** despacio que Juan.   You play **less** slowly **than** Juan.
Mi padre tiene **menos** hermanos que el tuyo.
My father has **fewer** brothers **than** yours.

Here's a variation for when you're comparing how actions are done.

Tu hermana habla **menos que** tú. Your sister speaks **less than** you.

'As ... as' is **tan/tanto ... como**

In English, to say that two things are equally tall, equally good, equally expensive, you say they are 'as ... as'. To say this in Spanish you use **tan ... como** for adjectives and adverbs and **tanto ... como** for nouns.

Here's the structure for when you're comparing qualities and how things are done.

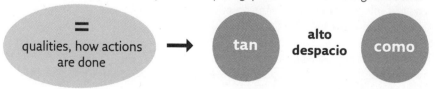

Yo soy **tan** alto **como** mi hermano.   I'm **as** tall **as** my brother. (male speaking)
Ella es **tan** alta **como** tú.   She's **as** tall **as** you.
Tú juegas **tan** despacio **como** Juan.   You play **as** slowly **as** Juan.

Here's a variation for when you're comparing how many things you have.

Tanto agrees in gender and number with the noun that goes with it.

Tengo **tanto** dinero **como** tú. I have **as much** money **as** you.
Bebemos **tanta** leche **como** vosotros. We drink **as much** milk **as** you.
Mi padre tiene **tantos** hermanos **como** el tuyo.
My father has **as many** brothers **as** yours.
Mi ciudad tiene **tantas** universidades **como** la tuya.
My city/town has **as many** universities **as** yours.

And here's a variation for when you're comparing how actions are done:
    Juan trabaja **tanto como** tú. Juan works **as much as** you (do).

Mental gymnastics 1

Look at the sign in brackets (**+**, **-** or **=**) and say what's missing:

más/menos ... que, tan/tanto/tanta/tantos ... como, más/menos que.

1   Estos pantalones son .... caros .... estos (+)
2   Tenemos .... trabajo .... vosotros. (=)
3   Mi hija es .... alta .... la tuya. (+)
4   Pagamos .... vosotros. (=)
5   Mis padres viajan .... ahora .... antes (-).
6   Mi ordenador es .... bueno .... el suyo. (=)
7   Tienes .... hijos .... yo. (-)
8   Estos atletas corren .... estos. (-)
9   Londres tiene .... habitantes .... Madrid (+)
10 Eva tiene .... paciencia .... yo. (=)

Mental gymnastics 2

Which Spanish word would you choose for the English word(s) in bold?

1   He speaks **as** fluently **as** her now.
    a   tanto   b   tan ... como   c   tanta ... como
2   You have **less** talent **than** our brother!
    a   menos que   b   menos ... que   c   tanto como
3   I feel **more** confident now.
    a   más   b   menos   c   tan
4   Paul studies **as** much **as** his brother.
    a   tanto ... como b   tanto como   c   tan como
5   They had **less** trouble **than** us!
    a   más que   b   menos ... que   c   tanto como
6   She has **more** power **than** the Prince.
    a   menos...que   b   tanto .. como   c   más ... que
7   You have **as many** shoes **as** a shoe shop!
    a   tantos ... como b   tantos como   c   tantas ... como

Irregular comparisons

As in English, some comparative words are irregular, such as **good** which becomes **better**.

bueno/a good	becomes	**mejor** better
buenos/as good	becomes	**mejores** better
malo/a bad	becomes	**peor** worse
malos/as bad	becomes	**peores** worse
*****grande** big	becomes	**mayor** older
*****grandes** big	becomes	**mayores** older
*****pequeño/a** small	becomes	**menor** younger
*****pequeños/as** small	becomes	**menores** younger

***mayor/mayores**, **menor/menores** normally refer to age rather than the height of a person:

Mi madre es **mayor** que mi padre. My mother is older than my father

but

Tu casa es más **grande** que la mía. Your house is bigger than mine.

bien well	becomes	**mejor** better
mal bad	becomes	**peor** worse

Careful!
Do not use **bueno** (good) for **bien** (well) or **malo** (bad) for **mal** (badly).

Mental gymnastics 3

Solve these anagrams and match the adjectives with their comparative forms.

1	JOMER	a	RANEDG ....
2	ENMOERS	b	LAOM ....
3	ROEP	c	NBEOU ....
4	YAROM	d	QPUSEOEÑ ....

Mental gymnastics 4

Reorder the sentences to find some comparisons.

1 estas – mejores – truchas – son – estas – que

....

2 que – vacaciones – tenemos – menos – vosotros

....

3 Pedro – que – gana – Marta – más

....

4 Julia – que – mayor – Emilia – es

....

5 tú – lentamente – que – más – trabajo

....

6 peor – cantas – que – yo

....

7 Mi – menor – es – el – hijo – tuyo – que

....

The cleverest of all

In Spanish, to express ideas such as 'the cleverest', 'the most' and 'the least', the definite article (**el**, **la**, **los** or **las**) followed by **más** (most) or **menos** (least) and the corresponding adjective, plus **de** is used. This allows a person or thing to be identified as having a quality in its highest or lowest degree amongst a group.

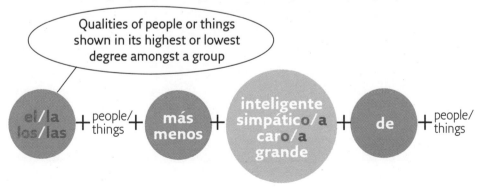

The article (**el**, **la**, **los**, **las**) and the adjective agree in gender and number with the gender or number of the person or thing being described.

El Everest es la montaña más alta del mundo.
Mount Everest is the tallest mountain in the world.

Irregular forms

Use the same irregular comparative forms which you learnt on the previous page to say 'the best', 'the worst', and so on.

bueno/a good	becomes	**el/la mejor** the best
buenos/as good	becomes	**los/las mejores** the best
malo/a bad	becomes	**el/la peor** the worst
malos/as bad	becomes	**los/las peores** the worst
grande big	becomes	**el/la mayor** the oldest
grandes big	becomes	**los/las mayores** the oldest
pequeño/a small	becomes	**el/la menor** the youngest
pequeños/as small	becomes	**los/las menores** the youngest

Mental gymnastics 5

How would you say in Spanish:

1   My sister Emilia is the oldest in the family.

....

2   Your omelette is the best in the world!

....

3   This hotel is the worst hotel in the city.

....

4   These sculptures are the most beautiful in the museum.

....

5   This film is the most interesting film of the year.

....

6   That photograph is the most expensive.

....

How to intensify the meaning of an adjective

To intensify the meaning of an adjective just put the word **muy** (very) before the adjective.

Es un hombre muy atractivo. He is a **very** attractive man.

or add **–ísimo, –ísima, –ísimos, –ísimas** to the end of the adjective. These endings convey the idea of 'very', 'extremely'. Choose the form taking into account whether the person or thing described is masculine or feminine, singular or plural.

• If the adjective ends in a consonant just add **–ísimo, –ísima, –ísimos, –ísimas**:
  difícil → dificil**ísimo/a/os/as**

Notice that the accent changes position.

• If the adjective ends in a vowel, remove the vowel and add **–ísimo, –ísima, –ísimos, –ísimas**:
  grande → grand**ísimo/a/os/as**

Note the spelling changes with adjectives ending in **–co, –go** or **–z**:

rico rich	ri**quísimo**,-a, –os, –as
largo long	lar**guísimo**, –a, –os, –as
feliz happy	feli**císimo**, –a, –os, –as

Mental gymnastics 6

Write sentences as in the example:

El tango es muy difícil.   **El tango es dificilísimo.**

1	La comida está muy salada.	....
2	Este camino es muy largo.	....
3	Tu novio es muy guapo.	....
4	Este libro es muy interesante.	....
5	El tiempo está muy seco.	....
6	Es una ciudad muy bella.	....

How to talk about what has or hasn't happened

17

So, what have you done?

In English, you can talk about the past like this:
'I **have worked** all afternoon' and 'This week **I have been** to Mexico.'

or like this:
'**I got up** late this morning'; '**We went** to the museum this afternoon.'
In Spanish these are both expressed in the same way, using the
perfect tense (G).

Perfect tense
You need two words to make the perfect tense:
• the present of the **verb** (G) **haber** (to have)
• a **past participle** (G): a verb form such as 'lived', 'spoken'

I **have worked** all afternoon
(Yo) **he** trabajado toda la tarde

We **went** to the museum this morning
(Nosotros) **hemos** ido al museo esta tarde

It goes like this:

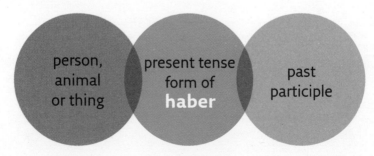

person, animal or thing — present tense form of **haber** — past participle

Past participle

In English, past participles are forms of the verb such as **written**, **spoken**, or **worked**, as in 'I have **written** a letter'.

How are past participles made up in Spanish?

Most verbs have an ending specific to their family:
the ending for **-AR** verbs is **-ado**
the ending for **-ER** & **-IR** verbs is **-ido**

As with the **present tense** (G), you just:

1   take the ending off the **infinitive** (G),
    e.g. for **hablar**, the **-ar** bit → **habl-**

ar

2   add the past participle ending → **habl-ado** → **hablado**

and that's it, you have a past participle in Spanish!

Mental gymnastics 1

Complete the past participles of the following verbs:

**salir • hablar • haber • estudiar • ser • beber • vivir
comer • recibir • cerrar • tener • estar**

1	habl-...............	7	s-..................
2	ten-................	8	est-................
3	viv-................	9	hab-...............
4	estudi-...........	10	cerr-.............
5	beb-...............	11	recib-...........
6	com-...............	12	sal-...............

Irregular past participles

In Spanish there are some common **irregular past participles** that you need to learn. Here are some of the most important:

abrir	to open	**abierto**	**cubrir**	to cover	**cubierto**
decir	to say	**dicho**	**escribir**	to write	**escrito**
hacer	to do, to make	**hecho**	**morir**	to die	**muerto**
poner	to put	**puesto**	**romper**	to break	**roto**
ver	to see	**visto**	**volver**	to come back	**vuelto**

Use the verb wheel to practise and use associations to memorise them.

Mental gymnastics 2

Fill in the missing letters to complete these irregular past participles.

1 e..... .....ri.....o
2 a.....ie..... .....o
3 .....uel.....o
4 .....i.....to

5 .....i..... .....o
6 .....o.....o
7 .....ec.....o
8 .....ue..... .....o

Perfect tense: summary

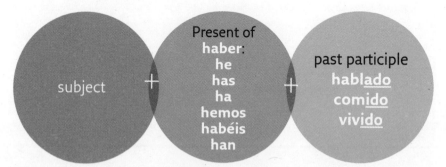

To make the perfect tense of the **reflexive verbs** (G) you learnt in Unit 14 you also use the verb **haber** and the **past participle** of the verb. The important thing to remember here is that the reflexive bit goes <u>before</u> **haber**:
me he levantado.   I got up.

Never put anything between **haber** and the **past participle**: these two words are 'crazy about each other', so do not separate them!

Mental gymnastics 3

Read the descriptions of people's moods below and match each description with one of the explanations given in bold below.

He encontrado un trabajo	**Hemos ido a un fiesta**
No han dormido bien	**Se ha levantado muy temprano**
Ha tenido muchas reuniones	**Hemos estado de vacaciones**

1   Vosotros estáis relajados. ....
2   Los niños están cansados. ....
3   El jefe está de mal humor. ....
4   ¡Estás contenta! ....
5   Marta está dormida. ....
6   Estáis de buen humor. ....

What hasn't happened

To talk about what hasn't happened, just put **no** before **haber**:
(yo) no he hablado con Laura. I didn't speak to Laura.
(nosotros) no hemos visitado el castillo. We didn't visit the castle.

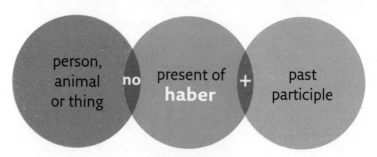

If the verb is reflexive put **no** before the reflexive bit:

Yo no me he levantado. I didn't get up.

Remember: **never** put anything between **haber** and the **past participle**: these two words are 'crazy about each other', so do not separate them!

Mental gymnastics 4

Rewrite the following sentences in the negative.

1   He visto a tu hermana esta tarde.

    ....

2   Juan se ha afeitado con tu crema.

    ....

3   ¿Habéis pagado la cena?

    ....

4   Hemos dormido bien.

    ....

5   Los niños han tenido clase hoy.

    ....

When to use the perfect tense

Use the perfect tense to refer to:

- completed past actions or events that are still having an effect in the present:

    No puedo salir porque **he perdido** las llaves del coche.
    I can't go out because I have lost the car keys.

- completed past actions or events, in a time frame that includes the present:

    ¿A qué hora **te has levantado** esta mañana?
    What time did you get up this morning?
    Este año **hemos viajado** mucho.
    This year we have travelled a lot.

Often the perfect tense appears with **time expressions** that include the present:

hoy	today
esta mañana/tarde/semana	this morning/afternoon/week
este mes/año/siglo	this month/year/century
recientemente	recently

Mental gymnastics 5

Join the beginnings of sentences on the left with the endings on the right to make some sentences in the past.

1	Pablo y Elena no	a	terminado el proyecto.
2	Esta semana ha	b	ido de vacaciones recientemente?
3	Habéis	c	hemos aprendido a cocinar.
4	Hoy yo no	d	han ido al cine.
5	¿Has	e	he hablado con Juan.
6	Este año	f	hecho frío.

How to talk about what happened

18

In Unit 17, you learnt how to talk about 'what has happened' – using the **perfect tense** (G – see Tense). In this unit, you'll learn about another past tense called the **preterite** (G – see Tense).

What did you do?

When you want to talk about what you did or what happened yesterday, last week or last century you say: 'Yesterday I **went** to the cinema', 'Last week we **had** a party', 'Last century mankind **walked** on the moon': **went**, **had** and **walked** are all forms of **verbs** (G) in the preterite and they express events or actions in the past that are completed and finished. As in English, Spanish uses verbs in the preterite to talk about events or actions that are viewed as over and done with.

To form the preterite you need the **stem** (G) of a verb and the endings of the preterite. Let's see how it is formed.

Preterite tense of regular verbs: using the correct ending
To create the correct form of the verb in Spanish, first take off the ending that you have found in the dictionar

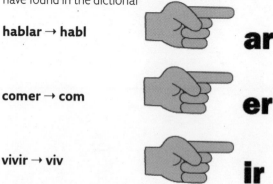

hablar → habl   **ar**

comer → com   **er**

vivir → viv   **ir**

Then add the endings to the bit you are left with, which is called the stem:
habl
com
viv

Each **yo**, **tú**, **él/ella/usted**, **nosotros/nosotras**, **vosotros/vosotras**, **ellos/ellas/ustedes** calls for a specific ending.

For example for **hablar**, the ending for **yo** is **-é**
(yo) **habl** + **é** = (yo) **hablé**   I spoke

For **comer**, the ending for **yo** is **-í**
(yo) **com** + **í** = (yo) **comí**   I ate

and for **vivir**, the ending for **yo** is **-í**
(yo) **vi** + **í** = (yo) **viví**   I lived

Let's look at the different types of regular verb (**G**):

1 the -AR type

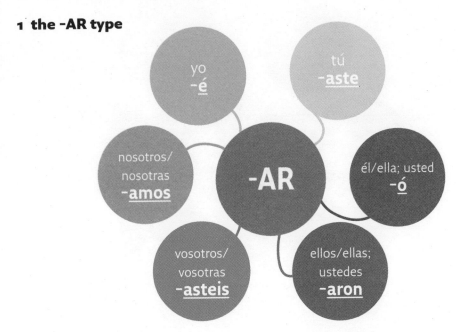

Notice that the **nosotros/nosotras** form is identical to the **present tense** (G) form; however, the context normally helps to make the meaning clear:

> Ayer compramos un coche.   Yesterday we bought a car.
> Hoy compramos un coche.   Today we're buying a car.

Go to the verb wheel accompanying this book and have a look at **acostarse** (to to go to bed), **hablar** (to speak, talk), **despertarse** (to wake up), **levantarse** (to get up) and **pensar** (to think). Remember that verbs such as **acostarse**, **despertarse** and **levantarse** are reflexive, so don't forget to include the reflexive bit: **me** acosté, **te** acostaste, **se** acostó, **nos** acostamos, **os** acostasteis, **se** acostaron.

2 the –ER and –IR types

Good news! The **–ER** and **–IR** types of regular verb have the same endings in the preterite.

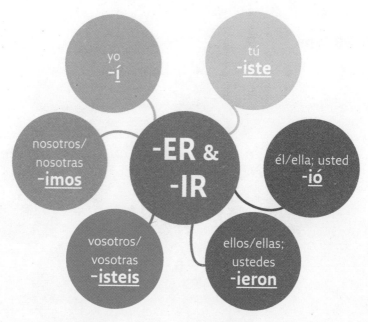

Notice that the **nosotros/nosotras** form of the **-ir** verbs is identical to the present tense form; however, as we saw above, the context normally helps to make the meaning clear:

Ayer salimos con Marina. Yesterday we went out with Marina
Hoy salimos con Marina. Today we're going out with Marina.

Try to recall these endings again in **two hours**, in **one day**, in **one week**, in **one month** and in **six months**.

Go to the verb wheel and have a look at **comer** (to eat), **conocer** (to know, meet), **entender** (to understand), **volver** (to return), **salir** (to go out, leave) and **vivir** (to live).

Mental gymnastics 1

Complete the following verbs with the correct endings.

1 yo habl–.....................................
2 ustedes gan–..........................
3 él estudi–.................................
4 nosotros escuch–....................

5 vosotros os despert–....................
6 ellas trabaj–................................
7 tú desayun–.................................
8 usted se levant–..........................

Mental gymnastics 2

Complete the words with their missing vowels. Verbs to look for in different forms: **comer**, **conocer**, **entender**, **volver**, **salir**, **vivir**, **decidir**. Don't forget the accents!

1 T SLST ....
2 VSTRS CMSTS ....
3 Y NTND ....
4 NSTRS VLVMS ....
5 STDS DCDRN ....
6 L V V ....
7 STD CNC ....

Mental gymnastics 3

Join the halves together to complete the verbs and add the correct subject (**yo**, **tú**, **él**, **nosotros**, **vosotros** or **ustedes**). For some there are several possible correct answers.

–imos   –ió   –dí   –eis   –te   –ron

1   .... apren–.........   4   .... vendis–.........
2   .... discutie–.........   5   .... cumpl–.........
3   .... respond–.........   6   .... escribist–.........

Verbs that undergo a spelling change in the preterite

Some verbs undergo a spelling change in the **yo** form. Let's take a look at them:

Yo form spelling change. Verbs ending in:

–gar: change **g** to **gu**
pag**ar** (to pay) → pa**gu**é, pagaste, pagó, pagamos, pagasteis, pagaron

–car: change **c** to **qu** – practi**car** (to practise) → practi**qu**é, practicaste, practicó, practicasteis, practicaron

–zar: change **z** to **c** – empe**zar** (to start) → empe**c**é, empezaste, empezó, empezamos, empezasteis, empezaron

–gar: **apagar** (to switch off), **jugar** (to play (a game)), **cargar** (to load), **negar** (to deny, refuse), **llegar** (to arrive), **pagar** (to pay) **pegar** (to stick, hit), **prolongar** (to prolong)
–car: **aparcar** (to park), **arrancar** (to pull, tear), **atacar** (to attack), **replicar** (to replicate), **sacar** (to take out), **tocar** (to touch, to play (a musical instrument))
–zar: **alcanzar** (to reach), **almorzar** (to have lunch), **analizar** (to analyse), **cruzar** (to cross), **gozar** (to enjoy, possess), **rozar** (to brush, rub)

Go to the verb wheel and have a look at **jugar** and **llegar**.

él/ella, usted,
ellos/ellas, ustedes forms
change their spelling

Some verbs change the **i** to **y**
leer → leí, leíste, le**y**ó, leímos, leísteis,
le**y**eron
notice the written accent over the letter **i**
oír → oí, oíste, o**y**ó, oímos, oisteis,
o**y**eron
verbs ending in **-uir**:
construir (to build) → construí,
construiste, constru**y**ó, construimos,
construisteis, constru**y**eron

caer (to fall), **creer** (to believe), **poseer** (to possess), **proveer** (to provide)
verbs ending in **-uir**: **contribuir** (to contribute), **destruir** (to destroy),
fluir (to flow), **incluir** (to include), **influir** (to influence)
Go to the verb wheel and have a look at **incluir**.

Mental gymnastics 4

Write the preterite form for **yo** of each of the following verbs.

1   apagar   3   analizar ....
2   aparcar   4   llegar ....

Mental gymnastics 5

Write the forms corresponding to **él/ella**, **usted**, **ellos/ellas**, **ustedes**
of the following verbs.

infinitive	él/ella; usted	ellos/ellas; ustedes
incluir		
creer		
destruir		
oír		

Mental gymnastics 6

How would you say the following in Spanish?

1   Yesterday I played tennis.   ....
2   We read your novel.   ....
3   Did he believe her?   ....
4   I didn't attack you.   ....
5   They built this house.   ....
6   You (formal, singular) replied well.   ....

Preterite tense of irregular verbs

There are a large number of verbs in Spanish that do not follow the rules for regular verbs as explained in Unit 9. These **irregular verbs** (G) are very common, so it's important that you try to learn how they work. As we did in the present tense, we are going to classify the irregular verbs into two groups to help you learn them:

- stem-changing verbs
- irregular verbs

In this unit you will learn the preterite of some of the most common irregular verbs. You will find lots of other irregulars on your verb wheel. Look at the wheel as you progress through this unit and use it to learn the irregular forms of the preterite. We will try to find patterns to help you remember these slightly more difficult verbs.

Preterite of stem-changing verbs

In Unit 10, we looked at a group of verbs whose stem changes in some forms. Remember, the stem is the bit you are left with after removing the **-ar**, **-er** or **-ir** ending of the basic form of a verb: **dormir** (to sleep) → **dorm-**.
There are two pieces of good news: the first is that in the preterite there are only **-ir** stem-changing verbs. The **-ar** and **-er** stem-changing verbs that you studied in Unit 10 are regular in the preterite: **pensar** (to think) (**pensé**, **pensaste** and so on), **entender** (to understand) (**entendí**, **entendiste** and so on).
The second piece of good news is the change in the stem only affects the **él/ella**, **usted**, **ellos/ellas**, **ustedes** forms. Let's take a look at the forms of the **-ir** stem-changing verbs. These verbs are grouped into two types:

Type 1: e → i

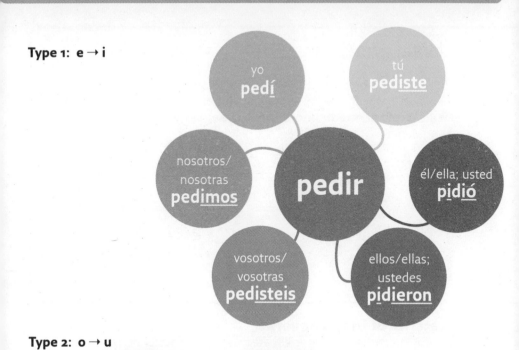

yo
ped**í**

tú
ped**iste**

nosotros/
nosotras
ped**imos**

pedir

él/ella; usted
p**i**d**ió**

vosotros/
vosotras
ped**isteis**

ellos/ellas;
ustedes
p**i**d**ieron**

Type 2: o → u

yo
dorm**í**

tú
dorm**iste**

nosotros/
nosotras
dorm**imos**

dormir

él/ella; usted
d**u**rm**ió**

vosotros/
vosotras
dorm**isteis**

ellos/ellas;
ustedes
d**u**rm**ieron**

ciento diecisiete 117

Mental gymnastics 7

Complete the words with their missing vowels. Work out the subject, then look for the following verbs in different forms: **competir**, **corregir**, **elegir**, **preferir**, **medir**, **morir**, **repetir**, **seguir**, **vestir**.

1	T RPTST	....
2	NSTRS CMPTMS	....
3	LLS CRRGRN	....
4	Y MD	....
5	L MR	....
6	STD SG	....
7	T VSTST	....
8	STDS LGRN	....
9	LL PRFR	....

Preterite of irregular verbs

Many of the commonly used verbs have irregular preterite forms. You are advised to learn them by heart if you can as you will need to use them often.

The following four verbs do not follow a pattern: **dar** (to give), **ir** (to go), **ser** (to be) and **ver** (to watch, to see). Have a look at them on the verb wheel.

Notice that **ir** and **ser** have identical forms in the preterite; however, you will be able to work out which one is being used because the context will make it clear:

Ayer fui a ver mi tía.	Yesterday I went to see my aunt.
Yo fui profesor de inglés.	I was an English teacher.

Mental gymnastics 8

Give yourself a few minutes to learn the forms of **dar**, **ir/ser** and **ver** and then complete the table. Remember, **ir** and **ser** have identical forms.

subject	dar	ir/ser	ver
yo	di		vi
tú			
él/ella; usted		fue	
nosotros/nosotras			
vosotros/vosotras			
ellos/ellas; ustedes			

Preterite of the other irregular verbs

Most of the other irregular verbs have an irregular stem but common endings. Some useful ones are:

infinitive	stem	endings	
estar (to be)	**estuv–**	e	(yo)
poder (to be able to)	**pud–**	iste	(tú)
poner (to put, to set)	**pus–**	o	(él/ella; usted)
querer (to want, to love)	**quis–**	imos	(nosotros/nosotras)
saber (to know)	**sup–**	isteis	(vosotros/vosotras)
tener (to have)	**tuv–**	ieron	(ellos/ellas; ustedes)
venir (to come)	**vin–**		

Notice:
- the ending for the **ellos/ellas**, **ustedes** form of verbs with a stem ending in **j-** is **-eron** (rather than **-ieron**):

conducir (to drive)	conduj-		condujeron
decir (to say)	dij-	**eron**	dijeron
producir (to produce)	produj-		produjeron
traducir (to translate)	traduj-		tradujeron

- the stem of **hacer** (to do, to make) is **hic-** but the form for **usted**, **él/ella** is **hiz-**: hice, hiciste, hizo, hicimos, hicisteis, hicieron

- the preterite of **hay** (**haber**: there is/are) is **hubo** (there was/were)

Go to the verb wheel and look at **conducir**, **decir**, **estar**, **poder**, **poner**, **querer**, **saber**, **tener** and **venir**.

Mental gymnastics 9

Solve these anagrams to find some more irregular verbs.

1. OY USQIE ....
2. SOOTORSV TUISTEVISES ....
3. LLESO UITERNOV ....
4. SUETD NIVO ....
5. SROSOOTN JIIOMSD ....
6. LALE DPUO ....
7. LELSA CJONNUEDRO ....
8. LÉ SOPU ....
9. RVSOATSO PISUSISTE ....
10. LLEA ZOIH ....

Mental gymnastics 10

Write the verb in brackets in the appropriate form of the preterite.

1   Ella no .... ir. (poder)
2   Ayer .... la noticia (saber, yo)
3   Federico y Ana .... el partido de tenis con nosotros. (ver)
4   Ellos .... la novela al inglés. (traducir)
5   Nosotros .... muy ocupados. (estar)
6   ¿Por qué no .... nuestro ordenador? (querer, tú)
7   Jaime .... la cena. (hacer)
8   Ellos nos .... el dinero. (dar)

When to use the preterite

Use the preterite to refer to:
● completed past actions or events that are viewed as over and done with.

Ayer conocí a tu hermano.   Yesterday I met your brother.
El año pasado fuimos a Brasil.   Last year we went to Brazil.

Often the **preterite** appears with <u>time expressions</u> such as:
ayer yesterday   **anoche** last night
hace dos días/años two days/years ago   **la semana pasada** last week
el mes/el año pasado last month/year   **el otro día** the other day

● a series of events that follow one another.

Ayer llegué a casa a las diez, hice la cena, me duché y me acosté.
Yesterday I arrived home at 10 o' clock, I made dinner, I had a shower and
I went to bed.

● the beginning of an action.

Empecé a trabajar hace diez años.   I started to work ten years ago.
Mi marido empezó a bailar a los   My husband started dancing at 18
18 años.   years of age.

Mental gymnastics 11

How would you say the following in Spanish?

1   I finished the book last night.
    ....

2   The other day we saw your father.
    ....

3   Last month Carlos was in London.
    ....

4   Did you (plural, informal) arrive ten days ago?
    ....

5   Did you (singular, informal) come with him yesterday?
    ....

How to describe situations in the past

In Units 17 and 18, you learnt how to talk about specific past events: 'what has happened' or 'what happened'. In this unit, you'll learn how to say 'how things used to be', 'what was going on' and to describe 'how things were'.

What was going on?

In English:

- to talk about 'how things used to be', you could say '**I used to go** to the gym every day', '**He used to come** to the beach with us at the weekend', 'Before, **they used to listen** to music all the time'
- to talk about 'what was going on', you might say 'When **I was living** in England, **I had** a big house' and
- to describe 'how things were', you could say 'A century ago, **the weather was** colder', 'When **my mother was** 18 years old, **she was** very beautiful'

'**I used to**', '**I was living**', '**I had**', '**the weather was**', '**when my mother was**', '**she was**' express actions, events or states that were happening or going on in the past and so, in the context of the sentence, these events, actions or states are not finished or completed.

Spanish has a tense called the **imperfect tense** (**G** – see Tense) to describe situations or habitual actions in the past. To form the imperfect tense you need the **stem** (**G**) of a **verb** (**G**) and an imperfect ending:

Imperfect tense of regular verbs: using the correct ending

To create the correct form of the verb in Spanish, first take off the ending that you have found in the dictionary:

hablar → habl

comer → com

vivir → viv

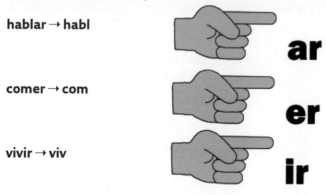

ar

er

ir

Then add the endings to the bit you are left with, which is called the stem:
habl
com
viv

Each **yo, tú, usted, el/ella, nosotros/nosotras, vosotros/vosotras, ustedes, ellos/ellas** calls for a specific ending.

For example for **hablar**, the ending for **yo** is **-aba**
(yo) **habl** + **aba** = (yo) **hablaba**   I used to speak

For **comer**, the ending for **yo** is **-ía**
(yo) **com** + **ía** = (yo) **comía**   I used to eat

and for **vivir**, the ending for **yo** is **-ía**
(yo) **vi** + **ía** = (yo) **vivía**   I used to live

Let's look at each of the verb types:

1. the -AR type

Here are the endings for the regular **-AR** verbs:

Hereis a reminder of some useful **-AR** verbs:

ahorrar to save	**colocar** to put, to place	**mostrar** to show
asar to roast	**comenzar** to start, to begin	**nadar** to swim
aterrizar to land	**despegar** to take off (e.g. a plane)	**organizar** to organise
caminar to walk	**enseñar** to teach, to show	**recordar** to remember
cocinar to cook	**llegar** to arrive	**terminar** to finish

Mental gymnastics 1

Take two minutes to memorise as many words as you can from the list above. Use your own memory techniques.

How many endings can you now recall without looking?

Mental gymnastics 2

Complete the following verbs in the imperfect.

enseñar • organizar • llegar • ahorrar • nadar • cocinar • terminar caminar

1 nosotros ahorr–.........................
2 usted organiz–.........................
3 yo camin–.........................
4 ella enseñ–.........................

5 vosotros nad–.........................
6 ellas lleg–.........................
7 tú cocin–.........................
8 ustedes termin–.........................

2. the -ER and -IR types

Good news! The **-ER** and **-IR** verbs take the same endings:

Here is a reminder of some useful **-ER** and **-IR** verbs:

aten**der**	to attend	prohi**bir**	to prohibit
cre**er**	to believe	mo**rir**	to die
de**ber**	to owe, should	consu**mir**	to consume
escon**der**	to hide	permi**tir**	to permit, to allow
exten**der**	to extend	ocu**rrir**	to occur
na**cer**	to be born	exis**tir**	to exist
reha**cer**	to redo, remake	u**nir**	to unite, to join
tem**er**	to fear	insis**tir**	to insist

Mental gymnastics 3

Complete the words with their missing vowels to make the following verbs in the imperfect tense. Don't forget the accents!

consumir • permitir • deber • nacer • creer • morir • rehacer • unir

1	y.....	cr..... ....
2	v.....s.....tr.....s	r.....h.....c..... ....s
3	.....ll.....s	d.....b..... .....n
4	l	n.....c..... .....
5	.....ll.....	m.....r..... .....
6	t.....	p.....rm.....t..... .....s
7	.....st.....d.....s	c.....ns.....m..... .....n
8	.....st.....d	.....n..... .....

The three irregular verbs: ir, ser, ver

subject pronouns	ir (to go)	ser (to be)	ver (to see, to watch)
yo	iba	era	veía
tú	ibas	eras	veías
él/ella; usted	iba	era	veía
nosotros/nosotras	íbamos	éramos	veíamos
vosotros/vosotras	ibais	erais	veíais
ellos/ellas; ustedes	iban	era	veía

Tony's Tip

Learn these three irregular verbs by heart: you could make each verb into a song to remember them. You can also use the verb wheel to test your knowledge.

Try to recall them again in **two hours**, in **one day**, in **one week**, in **one month** and in **six months**. The more you repeat them, the longer you will remember them.

How things used to be

Use the imperfect to talk about habitual actions in the past.

Antes jugaba al tenis todos los domingos.
Before, I used to play tennis every Sunday.
De niña, siempre iba a Escocia a casa de mi tía Moira.
When I was a girl, I always used to go to Scotland to stay at my aunt Moira's house.

The following expressions often appear with the imperfect tense when talking about habitual actions in the past:

siempre	always	**muchas veces**	often
frecuentemente	frequently	**cada año/día/mes**	every year/month
a menudo	often	**antes**	before

Mental gymnastics 4

Using the prompts below, join the halves together to complete the verbs. Then write **yo, tú, él** and so on as appropriate.

-aban -amos -ía -ían -a -ían -aba -abas

1 .... ib-.................... I used to go ...
2 .... cocin-.................... She used to cook ...
3 .... ér-.................... We used to be ...
4 .... prohib-.................... They used to prohibit ...
5 .... enseñ-.................... You (informal) used to teach ...
6 .... viv-.................... He used to live ...
7 .... ve-.................... You (formal, plural) used to watch ...
8 .... lleg-.................... They used to arrived ...

Use the imperfect to:
- talk about actions that were going on in the past:
  caminaba   I was walking
  hablaban   they were talking
  Entonces Julio trabajaba en Madrid.
  At that time (literally 'then'), Julio was working in Madrid.

- describe how people, animals and things were in the past:
  Mi profesor de matemáticas era muy simpático. My maths teacher was very nice.
  La casa de mis padres era muy grande. My parents' house was very big.
  La playa era pequeña. The beach was small.

Mental gymnastics 5

Rewrite the following sentences in the past.

1   Nosotros vamos al cine los viernes. ....
2   Mi perro es muy viejo. ....
3   Están muy contentos con su coche nuevo. ....
4   Mi marido siempre llega tarde de trabajar. ....
5   Tú eres un niño difícil. ....
6   El tiempo es frío y desagradable. ....
7   Yo tengo clase los lunes. ....
8   Mi mujer no desayuna nunca. ....

Imperfect or preterite?

To choose which tense to use, ask yourself the following questions:

- **Habitual or completed action in the past?**
  To refer to habitual actions in the past that occurred during an unspecified period of
  time, always choose the imperfect:
  Los lunes siempre terminaba de trabajar a las ocho de la tarde.
  On Mondays I always finished work at eight o'clock in the evening.

  However, if an action in the past occurred during a specific period of time and then
  ended, always choose the preterite (Unit 18):

Pero aquel lunes terminé de trabajar a las cinco de la tarde.
But that Monday I finished work at five o'clock in the afternoon.

- **Description or narration?**

  To describe a <u>situation</u> in the past, always choose the **imperfect** but to narrate events in the past, choose the **preterite**:

  Marta llegó a su casa, abrió la puerta y entró. De repente, vio a un hombre en la cocina. El hombre era alto y fuerte, tenía un revólver en la mano ...
  Marta arrived home, opened the door and went in. Suddenly, she saw a man in the kitchen. The man was tall and strong, he had a revolver in his hand ...

- **Interrupted or completed?**

  When one action is interrupted by another, the **imperfect** tense is **followed by** the **preterite**.

  Salía de mi casa, cuando me encontré con un amigo.
  I was coming out of my house when I bumped into a friend.

Mental gymnastics 6

Write the verbs in brackets either in the imperfect or the preterite.

Take care with the words marked with an asterisk: should their verbs be singular or plural?

1   Teresa .... (tomar) un café en el bar de Paco cuando
    .... (llegar) la policía*.
2   En verano siempre .... (ir) a casa de mis abuelos pero ese
    verano no .... (poder) ir.
3   Mi pueblo .... (ser) muy agradable. La gente* ....
    (ser) alegre y amable.
4   Entonces .... (vivir, yo) en Londres en un piso pequeño.
5   Paz .... (tener) 30 años cuando .... (casarse).
6   Antonio .... (bailar) muy bien pero .... (romperse)
    una pierna y .... (dejar) de bailar.

Mind Map it!

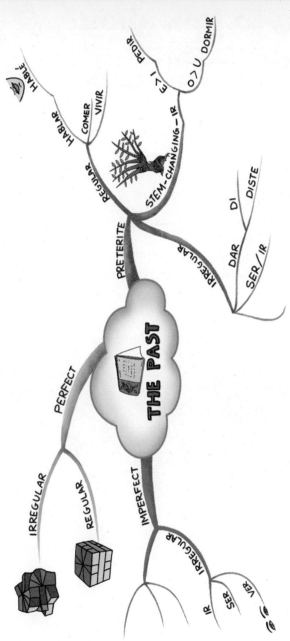

How to talk about future events 20

In this unit, you'll learn how to talk about future events.
In Spanish there are several ways to talk about what you
'are going to do' or 'will do'.

Planned events

In Spanish, as in English, when you talk about planned events you can use the
present tense (G).

Esta tarde tengo una reunión.   This afternoon I have a meeting.
Mañana voy al dentista.   Tomorrow I'm going to the dentist's.

Going to
In English, you can talk about the immediate future like this:
'I**'m going to** dance tonight' or 'she**'s going to** take the bus'.
The order of words is generally:

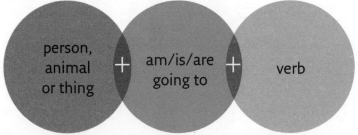

person, animal or thing + am/is/are going to + verb

The Spanish equivalent
The Spanish equivalent follows a similar pattern. You need to use **ir** (to go), followed
by **a** and an **infinitive** (G) (the basic frm of the verb). Look on your verb wheel to
remind yourself how **ir** works.

I **am going to** dance tonight
(Yo) **voy a** bailar **esta noche**

She **is going to** take the bus
(Ella) va a coger el autobús

The order of words looks like this:

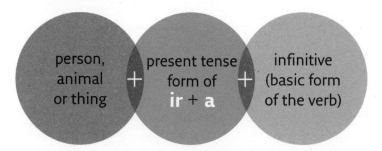

Forget about am, is or are
Remember: use **ir** only. Literally in Spanish, you say 'I go to call', 'she goes to take the bus' – so you don't need the 'am' of 'I am going'.

So rather than saying 'am going to' you just use 'go':
'I go to eat dinner' rather than 'I'm going to eat dinner'.
'He goes to call his friend' rather than 'He is going to call his friend'.

Not going to
To talk about what you're **not** going to do, just put **no** before the **ir** form.
I am not going to dance tonight.   **(Yo) no voy a bailar esta noche.**
She's not going to take the bus.   **(Ella) no va a coger el autobús.**

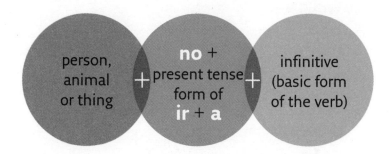

Mental gymnastics 1

Reorder the words to make some sentences that refer to the near future.

1 a – cine – esta – ir – tarde – al – voy

....

2 a – José – hoy – a – recoger – al – vamos – aeropuerto

....

3 el – vamos – a – a – la – sábado – playa – ir

....

4 a – vacaciones – ellos – ir – de – a – Londres – van

....

5 ¿vas – adónde – a – mañana – ir?

6 tren – las – va – el – salir – a – doce – a

....

What will be, will be

When you do something later or tomorrow you use the word 'will':
'I'**ll bring** some pizzas' or 'we **will go** to Canada next summer'.
This is called the **future tense** (G – see Tense).

In Spanish, the future tense works the same as the **present** (G) (Unit 9) and
imperfect (G) (Unit 19) tenses – you need 'I', 'you', 'he' or another **subject** (G)
and then the **verb** (G) with special endings.

Mental gymnastics 2

How would you say the following in Spanish?

1   Are you going to live in Paris? (informal, singular)

        ....

2   She's going to speak to her daughter.

        ....

3   We're going to watch a football match.

        ....

4   They're not going to sell their house.

        ....

5   I'm going to make a cake.

        ....

6   Are you going to go to his house? (informal, plural)

        ....

Building the future

Start off with the infinitive, the basic form of the verb you found in the dictionary –
but this time <u>don't</u> remove the ending. Instead, you add to it. Let's take a look:

    I **will bring** some pizzas.
    (Yo) **traeré** algunas pizzas.
    We **will go** to Canada next summer.
    (Nosotros) **iremos** a Canadá el verano que viene.

Start off with the infinitive: (**traer**, **ir)** then add the endings directly at the end.
traer → é → traeré
ir → é → iré

As for the present tense, each **yo**, **tú**,**él /ella**, **usted**, and so on calls for a specific
ending. Let's have a look at them:

Future endings

You'll be pleased to learn that the endings for regular **-AR**, **-ER** and **-IR** verbs are the same!

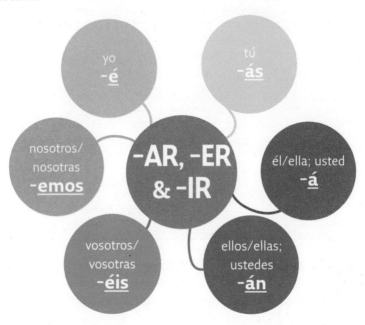

Mental gymnastics 3

Join the halves together to complete the words and match them with **yo**, **tú**, **él**, **nosotros**, **vosotros** or **ellos**.

-ás -ará -rán -aremos -éis -eré

1 .... com– .... 4 .... ir–....................
2 .... viaj– .... 5 .... ve–....................
3 .... pag– .... 6 .... escribir–....................

Irregular future forms

For some very common verbs, however, the future is **irregular** (G). They do not use the infinitive as the basis for making their future forms. Fortunately, you can find most of these forms on the verb wheel, which is a useful tool to help you memorise them. Let's just list some of the most useful verbs in this category:

caber (to fit, to be contained)	**cabr–**	
decir (to say, to tell)	**dir–**	
haber (to have)	**habr–**	
hacer (to do, to make)	**har–**	**–é**
poder (to be able)	**podr–**	**–ás**
poner (to put)	**pondr–**	**–á**
querer (to want, to love)	**querr–**	**–emos**
saber (to know)	**sabr–**	**–éis**
salir (to go out, to leave)	**saldr–**	**–án**
tener (to have)	**tendr–**	
valer (to be worth)	**valdr–**	
venir (to come)	**vendr–**	

Mental gymnastics 4

Solve these anagrams to make some irregular future forms.

1 LÉ RÁQEUR ....
2 SOOTRNOS ROSADEMSL ....
3 ÚT AÁRHS ....
4 LLSEO RNDIÁ ....
5 ROSOTOSV ÉDTNRISE ....
6 OY DPOÉR ....

What you won't do

To talk about what you won't do, just put **no** before the verb.

I won't come.	**No vendré.**
We won't visit the castle.	**No visitaremos el castillo.**

Mental gymnastics 5

Complete the puzzle below using future tense verbs.

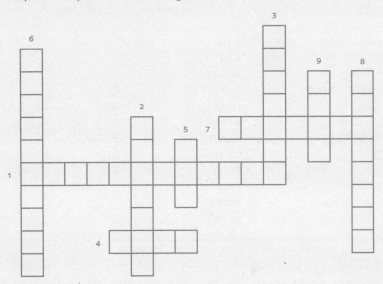

* Don't use any accents

Across

1   Nosotros... pronto (terminar)
4   Ella no ... el proyecto (hacer)
7   Ellas... venir (querer)

Down

2   Tú ... dinero (tener)
3   Vosotros ... hacerlo (poder)
5   Yo... el martes (ir)
6   Él... trabajo (encontrar)
8   Vosotros... el trofeo (ganar)
9   Usted ... el resultado en enero (ver)

Key to Mental Gymnastics and Glossary

Key to Mental Gymnastics

Unit 1

Mental gymnastics 1

padre – madre	toro – vaca
yerno – nuera	macho – hembra
marido – mujer	rey – reina
gallo – gallina	

Mental gymnastics 2

1. tía	5. intérprete
2. tenista	6. amiga
3. leona	7. estudiante
4. panda	8. perro

Mental gymnastics 3

masculine words	feminine words
2. problema	1. excursión
5. limón	3. terraza
6. doctor	4. universidad
7. cine	8. altitud
9. Pacífico	11. región
10. clima	13. cultura
12. garaje	14. profesora
16. biquini	15. sardina
17. inglés	18. diversidad

Mental gymnastics 4

masculine words	feminine words
amarillo	cantante
arroz	hermana
avión	mano
cantante	mesa
día	moto
libro	mujer
gato	niña
marido	noche
martes	cocina
problema	

Mental gymnastics 5

-s	-es	no change
ballenas	autobuses	miércoles
cafés	hindúes	
familias	hoteles	
mesas	limones	
taxis	mujeres	
	paces	

Mental gymnastics 6

1. abuelos	3. hijos
2. primos	4. tíos

Mental gymnastics 7

singular	plural	singular nouns referring to groups
persona	tijeras	ropa
perro	abuelos	familia
sal	zapatos	gente
sábado	menús	
hijo	gafas	
canguro		

Unit 2

Mental gymnastics 1

1. el	5. la	9. el	13. el
2. el	6. la	10. el	14. el
3. el	7. la	11. la	15. el
4. el	8. la	12. el	16. la

Mental gymnastics 2

1. una mujer	4. un problema
2. un caballo	5. una mano
3. una amiga	6. un coche

Key to Mental Gymnastics

Mental gymnastics 3
1. el hombre
2. una leona
3. el ratón
4. la persona
5. el agua
6. una universidad

Mental gymnastics 4
1. los amigos
2. la televisión
3. las bicicletas
4. las gafas de sol
5. el jamón
6. los jamones

Mental gymnastics 5
1. las noches
2. los jueves
3. los problemas
4. las personas
5. los melones
6. las fotos
7. los aviones

Mental gymnastics 6
1. unas personas
2. unos camiones
3. unas águilas
4. unos hoteles
5. unos días
6. unas vacas
7. unas motos

Mental gymnastics 7
1. un gato
2. una amiga
3. unos perros
4. una hija
5. unos sofás
6. unos estudiantes

Unit 3

Mental gymnastics 1
1. una gata bonita
2. una niña dormilona
3. una atleta joven
4. una mujer inteligente
5. una estudiante habladora

Mental gymnastics 2
1. nerviosa
6. difícil

2. impaciente
3. pesimista
4. alegre
5. trabajadora
7. optimista
8. atractiva
9. importante
10. feliz

Mental gymnastics 3
1. tranquilos
2. delgadas
3. organizadas
4. gordos
5. holgazanes
6. fuertes
7. capaces
8. intelectuales

Mental gymnastics 4
1. una ciudad interesante
2. una maleta redonda
3. un ratón gris
4. un hombre alto
5. un bebé grande
6. una actriz guapa

Mental gymnastics 5
1. a man
2. a woman
3. both
4. a woman
5. both
6. a man or a woman
7. both
8. a man or a woman

Unit 4

Mental gymnastics 1
1. vuestros zapatos
2. mi pantalón
3. su falda
4. tu calcetín
5. nuestra blusa
6. sus botas

Mental gymnastics 2
1. f
2. g
3. d
4. h
5. a
6. b
7. c
8. e

Key to Mental Gymnastics

Mental gymnastics 3
1. las fotos de él
2. las llaves de usted
3. los zapatos de ella
4. los hijos de ellos
5. los maridos de ellas

Mental gymnastics 4
1. el email/el correo electrónico de Claudia
2. la bicicleta de Pablo
3. el marido de mi hermana
4. los pisos de tus padres
5. los amigos de Elena

Mental gymnastics 5
1. nuestras amigas
2. sus hermanos
3. nuestros coches
4. mis hijos
5. vuestras motos
6. sus padres
7. tus tíos
8. nuestras motos

Mental gymnastics 6
1. nuestros amigos
2. su madre
3. vuestro hijo
4. su casa
5. sus sobrinos
6. tus padres
7. nuestras gatas
8. mis manos
9. vuestros coches
10. nuestro bebé
11. tu libro
12. mi profesor

Unit 5

Mental gymnastics 1
1. c
2. d
3. a
4. g
5. f
6. b
7. h
8. e

Mental gymnastics 2
1. la suya
2. los suyos
3. los nuestros
4. los míos
5. la tuya
6. el suyo
7. las suyas
8. la nuestra
9. los vuestros
10. los suyos

Mental gymnastics 3
1. la mía
2. el vuestro
3. la suya
4. las tuyas
5. el suyo
6. los nuestros

Mental gymnastics 4
1. la madre de ella
2. los zapatos de él
3. el billete de usted
4. el médico de ellas
5. los problemas de ustedes
6. los perros de ellos

Unit 6

Mental gymnastics 2

n	l	é	e	s	y	n	l
o	o	l	l	e	e	o	s
s	a	l	l	e	s	o	e
o	r	n	a	s	n	u	y
t	y	y	l	e	o	l	k
r	u	l	n	y	n	s	l
o	v	r	y	o	o	a	o
s	a	r	t	o	s	o	v

Mental gymnastics 3
1. ELLAS
2. NOSOTROS
3. ÉL
4. USTED
5. TÚ
6. VOSOTRAS
7. YO
8. ELLA

Mental gymnastics 4
1. usted
2. nosotros
3. tú
4. vosotros
5. él
6. ellas
7. usted
8. ustedes
9. ella
10. ellos
11. ellos
12. yo

Key to Mental Gymnastics

Unit 7
Mental gymnastics 2

Mental gymnastics 3
1. ELLOS SON
2. VOSOTROS SOIS
3. USTED ES
4. YO SOY
5. NOSOTROS SOMOS
6. TÚ ERES

Mental gymnastics 4
1. Juan es — de Barcelona.
2. Este zumo es — de naranja.
3. Sus tíos son — abogados.
4. El salón es — grande y luminoso.
5. La cama es — de madera.
6. Mis perros son — preciosos.
7. Su jefa es — exigente.
8. Hoy es — lunes.
9. ¿Cuánto es — el café?
10. Nosotros somos — australianos.
11. El reloj es — redondo.
12. La novela es — aburrida y larga.
13. Yo soy — británica.
14. Vosotras, ¿sois — hijas de Dolores?

Mental gymnastics 5
Masculine version:
Yo soy español, soy de Málaga. Soy una persona agradable, paciente, optimista y trabajadora. No soy guapo, soy alto y delgado. Soy fotógrafo. Soy hijo de un pintor y una profesora y nieto de un arquitecto importante de Málaga. Mi casa es de madera y es antigua. Es grande y el salón es bonito y original.

Feminine version:
Yo soy española, soy de Málaga. Soy una persona agradable, paciente, optimista y trabajadora. No soy guapa, soy alta y delgada. Soy fotógrafa. Soy hija de un pintor y una profesora y nieta de un arquitecto importante de Málaga. Mi casa es de madera y es antigua. Es grande y el salón es bonito y original.

Mental gymnastics 6
1. Jaime es de Chile.
2. El sofá es de piel.
3. Es la una y media.
4. Hoy es miércoles.
5. Ellos son aburridos.
6. Nosotros no somos ingleses, somos escoceses.
7. Mi madre es enfermera.
8. El amigo de Samuel es inteligente.
9. El dinero es para Carlos.
10. El cuchillo es para cortar la tortilla.

Unit 8
Mental gymnastics 2
1. ÉL ESTÁ
2. USTEDES ESTÁN
3. VOSOTROS ESTÁIS
4. YO ESTOY
5. NOSOTROS ESTAMOS
6. TÚ ESTAS

Mental gymnastics 3
1. Mis suegros están de vacaciones en Cuba.
2. Las llaves están en mi bolso.
3. Manchester está cerca de Liverpool.
4. Granada está a dos horas de mi casa.
5. Tengo fiebre, estoy enfermo.
6. Estamos cansados, trabajamos mucho.
7. El color rojo está de moda.

8. El museo está cerrado los lunes.
9. Mis hijos están contentos.
10. El señor García no está, está de viaje.
11. Estoy cansado de estar de pie.
12. El coche está roto.

Mental gymnastics 4
1. ¿Está Laura de vacaciones?
2. Las llaves están en la mesa.
3. La cocina está rota.
4. La sopa está muy caliente.
5. El jefe/La jefa está de mal humor.
6. Estoy en Barcelona.
7. Mi marido está de viaje.
8. El aeropuerto está cerca de la estación de tren.
9. Mi casa está a 20 km (kilómetros) de la playa.
10. Las vacaciones en España están de moda.

Unit 9
Mental gymnastics 2
1. nosotros habl**amos**
2. ustedes pag**an**
3. él limpi**a**
4. yo compr**o**
5. vosotros alquil**áis**
6. ellas trabaj**an**
7. tú estudi**as**
8. usted cen**a**

Mental gymnastics 3
1. TÚ METES
2. NOSOTROS BEBEMOS
3. YO COMO
4. VOSOTROS LEÉIS
5. USTED VENDE
6. ELLOS APRENDEN
7. ELLA RESPONDE

Mental gymnastics 4
1. yo cumplo
2. ustedes deciden
3. ella escribe
4. vosotros vivís
5. tú abres
6. nosotros subimos
7. tú divides
8. nosotros discutimos

Mental gymnastics 5

Unit 10
Mental gymnastics 4
1. yo corrijo
2. nosotros dormimos
3. ustedes prefieren
4. tú juegas/ella juega
5. vosotros volvéis
6. tú cierras/ella cierra

Key to Mental Gymnastics

Mental gymnastics 5
1. TÚ ENCIENDES
2. NOSOTROS PROBAMOS
3. ELLOS ELIGEN
4. YO MIDO
5. VOSOTROS RECORDÁIS
6. USTED ALMUERZA
7. TÚ COMPITES
8. YO CIERRO

Mental gymnastics 2

	-tú	**nosotros**
decir	dices	decimos
saber	sabes	sabemos
ver	ves	vemos
salir	sales	salimos

Mental gymnastics 6

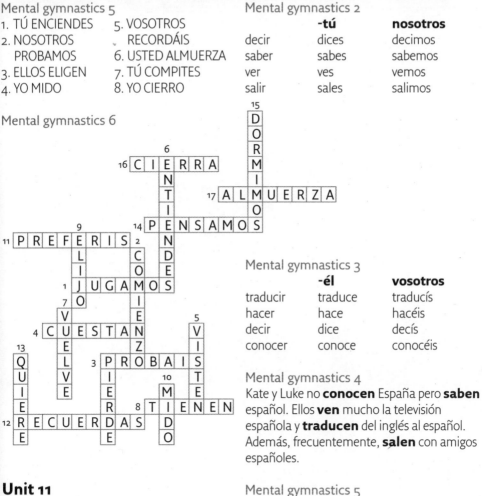

Mental gymnastics 3

	-él	**vosotros**
traducir	traduce	traducís
hacer	hace	hacéis
decir	dice	decís
conocer	conoce	conocéis

Mental gymnastics 4
Kate y Luke no **conocen** España pero **saben** español. Ellos **ven** mucho la televisión española y **traducen** del inglés al español. Además, frecuentemente, **salen** con amigos españoles.

Unit 11

Mental gymnastics 1
1. distribuyo
2. conozco
3. salgo
4. veo
5. sé
6. traduzco
7. hago
8. doy
9. agradezco
10. construyo

Mental gymnastics 5
1. YO OIGO
2. VOSOTROS DECÍS
3. ELLOS VIENEN
4. USTED TIENE
5. NOSOTROS DECIMOS
6. ELLA OYE
7. YO DIGO
8. ÉL VIENE

Key to Mental Gymnastics

Mental gymnastics 6
1. TÚ ERES
2. NOSOTROS HEMOS
3. ELLOS/ ELLAS ESTÁN
4. YO HE
5. VOSOTROS SOIS
6. YO ESTOY
7. TÚ VAS
8. YO SOY

Mental gymnastics 7
1. I do (practise) a lot of sport.
2. She knows how to make Spanish omelette.
3. We don't know your father.
4. Juan translates very well.
5. Do you know how to dance the salsa?
6. We're going to Madrid tomorrow.
7. I leave the house at 8.
8. I'm hot.

Mental gymnastics 8

9. Quiero aquélla.

Mental gymnastics 3
1. a   3. c   5. b   7. c   9. c
2. b   4. b   6. c   8. b   10. b

Mental gymnastics 4
1. No quiero eso ni esto, quiero **aquello**.
2. **Estos** estudiantes son inteligentes.
3. No quiero **ese** sombrero, quiero éste.
4. **Aquellas** casas son muy caras.
5. **Este** coche es de mi hermano.
6. **Esta** playa es maravillosa.
7. **Estos** problemas son difíciles.
8. **Esto** es interesante.
9. ¿Cuál quieres: éste, ése o **aquél**?
10. Ésas son feas, **ésas** son bonitas pero aquéllas son horribles.

Unit 12
Mental gymnastics 1
1. Eso es bueno.
2. No entiendo esto.
3. ¿Qué es aquello?
4. ¿Entiendes eso?
5. ¡Esto es terrible!

Mental gymnastics 2
1. este sofá   2. este ordenador   3. Quiero ésta.
4. esos amigos   5. Quiero ésa.   6. ese jersey
7. aquellas gafas de sol   8. aquellos limones

Unit 13
Mental gymnastics 1
1. ¿Usted es inglés?/¿Es usted inglés?
2. ¿Usted vive en Londres?/ ¿Vive usted en Londres?
3. ¿Eres estudiante?
4. ¿No trabajas?

Key to Mental Gymnastics

5. ¿Usted está de vacaciones?/
   ¿Está usted de vacaciones?
6. ¿No quieres tomar algo?
7. ¿Vives aquí?
8. Usted habla español?/
   ¿Habla usted español?

Mental gymnastics 2
1. ¿Vives en Londres?
2. ¿Tenéis hijos?
3. ¿Vives en un piso con tu novia?
4. ¿Vive tu familia en Nueva Zelanda?
5. ¿Estás casado?
6. ¿Trabajas en Manchester?

Mental gymnastics 3
1. CUÁL
2. POR QUÉ
3. CUÁNDO
4. QUÉ
5. CÓMO
6. DÓNDE
7. CUÁLES
8. CUÁNTO
9. ADÓNDE

Mental gymnastics 4
1. ¿De dónde eres?
2. ¿Adónde vas esta tarde?
3. ¿Cuántos hijos tienes?
4. ¿Por qué vas al aeropuerto?
5. ¿Cuánto es?
6. ¿Cuándo vienen tus amigos?
7. ¿Qué idiomas estudias?
8. ¿Cómo es tu novio?

Mental gymnastics 5
1. ¿Qué color prefieres?
2. ¿Cuál deseas? ¿Este o ese?
3. ¿Qué ciudad está en la costa?
4. ¿Cuáles son tus ciudades preferidas?
5. ¿Cuál es tu libro favorito?

Mental gymnastics 6
1. ¿Cuántos periódicos lees?
2. ¿Cuánta agua bebes?
3. ¿Cuántas amigas españolas tienes?
4. ¿Cuánto aceite quieres?
5. ¿Cuántos idiomas hablas?

Mental gymnastics 7
1. b   2. d   3. a   4. e   5. c

Unit 14

Mental gymnastics 1
1. f   2. h   3. d   4. c

5. b   6. e   7. g   8. a

Mental gymnastics 2
1. María se peina.
2. Tú te vistes.
3. Vosotros os maquilláis.
4. Juan y Pedro se afeitan.
5. Yo me acuesto.
6. Nosotros nos lavamos.

Mental gymnastics 3
1. me acuesto
2. viste
3. afeita
4. levantamos
5. os levantáis
6. acuesta

Unit 15

Mental gymnastics 1
1. Nosotros no hablamos español.
2. Nuestra casa no es grande.
3. El problema no está solucionado.
4. Ellos no tienen hambre.

Key to Mental Gymnastics

5. Yo no me peino bien.
6. Los niños no tienen frío.
7. No quiero visitar el museo.
8. No tenemos euros.
9. No nos vestimos rápido.
10. No hago la comida.

Mental gymnastics 2
1. No bebo nunca.
2. No está nada en su sitio.
3. No habla nadie.
4. No quiero café tampoco.
5. No está enfermo ninguno de los estudiantes.
6. No hace deporte ninguna persona.
7. No sabe nadie latín.

Mental gymnastics 3
1. Mi madre no come nunca a la una.
2. No entra nadie.
3. No quiero nada para el dolor de cabeza.
4. No habla inglés ninguna de mis amigas.
5. No tenemos nada.
6. Ninguno quiere tortilla.
7. No salgo los viernes nunca.
8. Hoy no viene ningún amigo a cenar.

Unit 16
Mental gymnastics 1
1. más ... que
2. tanto ... como
3. más ... que
4. tanto como
5. menos ... que
6. tan ... como
7. menos ... que
8. menos que
9. más ... que
10. tanta ... como

Mental gymnastics 2
1. b   3. a   5. b   7. a
2. b   4. b   6. c

Mental gymnastics 3
1. MEJOR   c. BUENO
2. MENORES   d. PEQUEÑOS
3. PEOR   b. MALO
4. MAYOR   a. GRANDE

Mental gymnastics 4
1. Estas truchas son mejores que estas.
2. Tenemos menos vacaciones que vosotros.
3. Pedro gana más que Marta.
4. Julia es mayor que Emilia.
5. Trabajo más lentamente que tú.
6. Cantas peor que yo.
7. Mi hijo es menor que el tuyo.

Mental gymnastics 5
1. Mi hermana Emilia es la mayor de la familia.
2. ¡Tu tortilla es la mejor del mundo!
3. Este hotel es el peor (hotel) de la ciudad.
4. Estas esculturas son las más hermosas/bonitas del museo.
5. Esta película es la (película) más interesante del año.
6. Esa fotografía es la más cara.

Mental gymnastics 6
1. La comida está saladísima.
2. Este camino es larguísimo.
3. Tu novio es guapísimo.
4. Este libro es interesantísimo.
5. El tiempo está sequísimo.
6. Es una ciudad bellísima.

Key to Mental Gymnastics

Unit 17

Mental gymnastics 1

Infinitive	past participle
1. hablar	hablado
2. tener	tenido
3. vivir	vivido
4. estudiar	estudiado
5. beber	bebido
6. comer	comido
7. ser	sido
8. estar	estado
9. haber	habido
10. cerrar	cerrado
11. recibir	recibido
12. salir	salido

Mental gymnastics 2

1. escrito	5. dicho
2. abierto	6. roto
3. vuelto	7. hecho
4. visto	8. muerto

Mental gymnastics 3

1. Vosotros estáis relajados. Hemos estado de vacaciones.
2. Los niños están cansados. No han dormido bien.
3. El jefe está de mal humor. Ha tenido muchas reuniones.
4. ¡Estás contenta! He encontrado un trabajo.
5. Marta está dormida. Se ha levantado muy temprano.
6. Estáis de buen humor. Hemos ido a un fiesta.

Mental gymnastics 4

1. No he visto a tu hermana esta tarde.
2. Juan no se ha afeitado con tu crema.
3. ¿No habéis pagado la cena?
4. No hemos dormido bien.
5. Los niños no han tenido clase hoy.

Mental gymnastics 5

1. d (Pablo y Elena no han ido al cine).
2. f (Esta semana ha hecho frío).
3. a (Habéis terminado el proyecto.)
4. e (Hoy yo no he hablado con Juan.)
5. b (¿Has ido de vacaciones recientemente?)
6. c (Este año hemos aprendido a cocinar.)

Unit 18

Mental gymnastics 1

1. yo habl**é**	5. vosotros os despert**asteis**
2. ustedes gan**aron**	6. ellas trabaj**aron**
3. él estudi**ó**	7. tú desayun**aste**
4. nosotros escuch**amos**	8. usted se levant**ó**

Mental gymnastics 2

1. TÚ SALISTE	5. USTEDES DECIDIERON
2. VOSOTROS COMISTEIS	6. ÉL VIVIÓ
3. YO ENTENDÍ	7. USTED CONOCIÓ
4. NOSOTROS VOLVIMOS	

Mental gymnastics 3

1. yo aprendí	4. tú vendiste
2. ustedes discutieron	5. él cumplió
3. nosotros respondimos	6. vosotros escribisteis

Key to Mental Gymnastics

Mental gymnastics 4

Infinitive	yo
apagar	apagué
aparcar	aparqué
analizar	analicé
llegar	llegué

Mental gymnastics 5

Infinitive	-él/ella; usted
incluir	incluyó
creer	creyó
destruir	destruyó
oír	oyó

ellos/ellas; ustedes

incluyeron
creyeron
destruyeron
oyeron

Mental gymnastics 6

1. Ayer jugué al tenis.
2. Nosotros leímos tu novela.
3. ¿La creyó?
4. Yo no te ataqué.
5. Ellos/Ellas construyeron esta casa.
6. Usted replica bien.

Mental gymnastics 7

1. TÚ REPETISTE
2. NOSOTROS COMPETIMOS
3. ELLOS/ELLAS CORRIGIERON
4. YO MEDÍ
5. ÉL MURIÓ
6. USTED SIGUIÓ
7. TÚ VESTISTE
8. USTEDES ELIGIERON
9. ELLA PREFIRIÓ

Mental gymnastics 8

subject	dar	ir/ser	ver
yo	di	fui	vi
tú	diste	fuiste	viste
él/ella; usted	dio	fue	vio
nosotros/ nosotras	dimos	fuimos	vimos
vosotros/ vosotros	disteis	fuisteis	visteis
ellos/ellas; ustedes	dieron	fueron	vieron

Mental gymnastics 9

1. YO QUISE
2. VOSOTROS ESTUVISTEIS
3. ELLOS TUVIERON
4. USTED VINO
5. NOSOTROS DIJIMOS
6. ELLA PUDO
7. ELLAS CONDUJERON
8. ÉL SUPO
9. VOSOTRAS PUSISTES
10. ELLA HIZO

Mental gymnastics 10

1. pudo	5. estuvimos
2. supe	6. quisiste
3. vieron	7. hizo
4. tradujeron	8. dieron

Mental gymnastics 11

1. Terminé el libro anoche.
2. El otro día vimos a tu padre.
3. El mes pasado Carlos estuvo en Londres.
4. ¿Lo supisteis hace diez días?
5. ¿Viniste con él ayer?

Key to Mental Gymnastics

Unit 19
Mental gymnastics 2
1. nosotros ahorr**ábamos**
2. usted organiz**aba**
3. yo camin**aba**
4. ella enseñ**aba**
5. vosotros nad**abais**
6. ellas lleg**aban**
7. tú cocin**abas**
8. ustedes termin**aban**

Mental gymnastics 3
1. yo creía
2. vosotros/vosotras rehacíais
3. ellos/ellas debían
4. él nacía
5. ella moría
6. tú permitías
7. ustedes consumían
8. usted unía

Mental gymnastics 4
1. Yo iba
2. ella cocinaba
3. nosotros/nosotras éramos
4. ellos/ellas prohibían
5. tú enseñabas
6. él vivía
7. ustedes veían
8. ellos/ellas llegaban

Mental gymnastics 5
1. Nosotros íbamos al cine los viernes.
2. Mi perro era muy viejo.
3. Estaban muy contentos con su coche nuevo.
4. Mi marido siempre llegaba tarde de trabajar.
5. Tú eras un niño difícil.
6. El tiempo era frío y desagradable.
7. Yo tenía clase los lunes.
8. Mi mujer no desayunaba nunca.

Mental gymnastics 6
1. Teresa tomaba un café en el bar de Paco cuando llegó la policía.
2. En verano siempre iba a casa de mis abuelos pero ese verano no pude ir.
3. Mi pueblo era muy agradable. La gente era alegre y amable.
4. Entonces vivía en Londres en un piso pequeño.
5. Paz tenía 30 años cuando se casó.
6. Antonio bailaba muy bien pero se rompió una pierna y dejó de bailar.

Unit 20
Mental gymnastics 1
1. Voy a ir al cine esta tarde./ Esta tarde voy a ir al cine.
2. Hoy vamos a recoger a José al aeropuerto.
3. Vamos a ir a la playa el sábado/ El sábado vamos a ir a la playa.
4. Ellos van a ir de vacaciones a Londres.
5. ¿Adónde vas a ir mañana?
6. El tren va a salir a las doce.

Mental gymnastics 2
1. ¿Vas a vivir en París?
2. Ella va a hablar con su hija.
3. Vamos a ver un partido de fútbol.
4. Ellos no van a vender su casa.
5. Voy a hacer un pastel.
6. ¿Vais a ir a su casa?

Mental gymnastics 3
1. yo comeré
2. nosotros viajaremos
3. él pagará
4. vosotros iréis
5. ellos verán
6. tú escribirás

Mental gymnastics 4
1. ÉL QUERRA
2. NOSOTROS SALDREMOS
3. TÚ HARÁS
4. ELLOS DIRÁN
5. VOSOTROS TENDRÉIS
6. YO PODRÉ

Mental gymnastics 5

Glossary

Adjective

Adjectives are words that describe nouns. When we say **Luis es alto y Sara es baja** the words **alto** and **baja** are telling us what Luis and Sara are like; they give us more information about them.

Adverb

Adverbs modify verbs, adjectives or other adverbs by saying how, when, where, how much or how often something is done or happens. Words like **bien** (well), **mañana** (tomorrow), **aquí** (here), **bastante** (enough) and **sencillamente** (simply) are adverbs.

Article

Articles are words that indicate if a noun is specific or non-specific. The **definite article** 'the' has four forms in Spanish: **el, la, los, las, el profesor de español** (the Spanish teacher). The **indefinite article** 'a/an, some' also has four forms: **un, una, unos** and **unas, un profesor de español** (a Spanish teacher).

Gender

A grammatical term which classifies a word either as **masculine** or **feminine**. All Spanish nouns (not only those which refer to people or animals) are either masculine or feminine: **casa** (house) feminine; **árbol** (tree) masculine.

Infinitive

The form of the verb with 'to' in front of it, e.g. to walk, to have, to be, to go. In Spanish, infinitives end in **–ar**, **–er** or **–ir**, e.g. **trabajar, beber, vivir**.

Interrogative

A word used to express a question, **¿Qué?** 'What?', **¿Dónde? 'Where?', ¿Cuándo?** 'When?' and so on, are all interrogative words: **¿Qué libro lees?** 'What book are you reading?', **¿Dónde vives?** 'Where do you live?', **¿Cuando llegas?** 'When do you arrive?'

Noun

Nouns are words for people, animals, things and even ideas, feelings or emotions: **mujer** (woman), **gato** (cat), **casa** (house), **democracia** (democracy), **miedo** (fear).

Number

A grammatical category which indicates whether something is **singular** or **plural**: **esta mujer es inteligente** (this woman is intelligent), **estas mujeres son inteligentes** (these women are intelligent).

Past participle

A past participle is a non personal form of the verb: **trabajado** (worked), **comido** (eaten), **dormido** (slept). When used with the verb **haber**, it forms compound tenses, such as the perfect tense: **hoy he trabajado en casa** (today I have worked at home). It can also be used as adjective: **la ventana está abierta** (the window is open).

Possessive

Possessives are words that indicate possession or ownership. They can be **adjectives**: **mi hermano** (my brother) or **pronouns:** **las bicicletas son nuestras** (the bicycles are ours).

Glossary

Preposition
Prepositions are words that link two other words or groups of words in order to indicate a relationship of time, space, possession, etc.: **Llegamos por la tarde** 'We arrive in the afternoon', **El libro está en la mesa** 'the book is on the table'

Present Participle
The present participle is the form of the verb that is used to say what is happening at the moment. It is invariable. In English, verbs ending in -ing are present participles and in Spanish -ando or -iendo: **en este momento estoy trabajando** (at the moment I am working).

Pronoun
A word that replaces or refers to a noun: **ella** (she), **el tuyo** (yours), **¿Quién?** (Who?) etc.

Reflexive verb
Verbs such as **me despierto** (I wake up), **te levantas** (you get up), that can express actions done by the subject for or to himself/herself, are said to be reflexive. These verbs are always accompanied by a reflexive pronoun: **me, te, se, nos, os, se** (myself, yourself, himself, etc.). Reflexive verbs are a large category in Spanish.

Stem
The part of a verb to which endings are added.

Subject Pronoun
A pronoun representing the person or thing that performs an action or exists in a state: **Ellas compraron un piso** (they bought a flat), **él es viejo** (he is old).

Subject
A word or group of words that perform an action or exist in a state: **Julia y Carlos compraron un coche** 'Marta and Lola bought a car', **el vestido es nuevo** 'the dress is new'.

Tense
The form of the verb which indicates the time of the action: past, present or future: **Present tense**: A verb form used to talk about what is true at the moment, what happens regularly and what is happening now; for example: I'm a student; I travel to college by train; I'm studying languages. **Perfect tense**: a verb form used to talk about what has or hasn't happened: I have spoken w͏ᵗ _____ ͏ense: A verb form use͏ _____ ͏ere complet͏ _____ corres͏ _____ English, for examp͏ie. _____ ͏oike; Mary went to the shops on Friday; I typed two reports yesterday. **Imperfect tense**: One of the tenses used to talk about the past, especially in descriptions, and to say what was happening or used to happen; e.g.: When I was a child, I used to go the beach everyday. **Future tense**: A tense used to talk about something that will happen or will be true.

Verb
A verb is a word that indicates an action or a state: **Juan estudia inglés** (Juan studies English), **Emilia es joven** (Emilia is young). Verbs can be: **regular** – verbs whose forms follow a pattern; **irregular** – verbs which do not follow a general pattern; or **stem-changing** – verbs which change their stem in certain tenses and in certain persons.